MAGELLAN PRESS PRESENTS

W9-DDG-681

A GUIDE TO THE BEST   RESTAURANTS IN AMERICA

WHERE THE LOCALS EAT™

NEW YORK

Editors/Writers: Pat Embry, Liz Garrigan,
Charles Harris, Catherine Johnson,
Rachel Lawson and Elizabeth Ramsey

Book Design: Brian Relleva

Web and Mobile: Byron McClain and Tom Mason

Restaurant Relations: Kelsey Weaver

Editorial Assistant: Gina Kuhn

MAGELLAN PRESS, INC.
Nashville, Tennessee
www.magellanpress.com

WWW.WHERETHELOCALSEAT.COM

Where the Locals Eat: New York

First Edition

Copyright © 2008.

Published by Magellan Press, Inc., P.O. Box 1167, Brentwood, Tennessee 37027. Printed in the United States of America.

Printed by Fidlar Doubleday, Inc., Davenport, Iowa

Library of Congress Control Number: 2008936313

ISBN: 978-1-928622-31-4

31-1-1-101908

WELCOME TO WHERE THE LOCALS EAT

A few words about what you'll find in the following pages, and we'll start with a confession: In most of the 50 cities we cover, finding the 100 best places to eat — which is our franchise — is difficult, but not impossible. In New York, no one can narrow the field of great restaurants to only 100.

So what we've done is to crown not only what we think are the city's **top 100 restaurants** but also recognize another 200 or so dining spots that we like to call our neighborhood favorites. And we've drilled down even farther: Among those, we'll tell you, for example, where to find the best burger on the Upper West Side and the best sushi in Brooklyn.

Besides those category winners we think are so important, here too are the undiscovered finds and the neighborhood spots you've never heard of, but which remain predictably packed with regulars. We've learned of the incomparable pizza at Ottimo and the delicious guacamole at Taco Taco. You won't find these in most other guides, but just ask around the Flatiron district or the Upper East Side, and you'll know why we're fans.

Sure, we gave the top 100 picks the most ink in the following pages, but don't overlook the shorter write-ups about places without which New York simply would not be the same.

The Editors
Magellan Press

THE BEST RESTAURANTS IN AMERICA

NEW YORK
NEW YORK

TABLE OF CONTENTS

RESTAURANTS BY
CATEGORY

★ denotes best in category

African

American Traditional

Asian Fusion

Australian

Austrian

Bagels

Bakery

CATEGORIES

5

6

Brunch

8

CATEGORIES

9

Buffet/Cafeteria

Burgers

10

Burritos

Café

Caribbean/Tropical

Cheese Steaks

Continental

Cuban

12

BOOK REVUE

3/4: Karamo Brown. *Queer Eye*'s culture expert & author of *Karamo*, 7pm "tickets required"

3/6: Today Show co-anchor Hoda Kotb. *You Are My Happy*, 7pm

3/7: Janice Dean, Fox & Friends Meteorologist, *Mostly Sunny*, 7pm

3/11: Long Island Writers Guild writing workshop - no need to register - 7pm

3/29: Book Revue Book Group discusses *The Ninth Hour* - 7pm

3/24 Long Island Writers Guild Reads open mic event, no signup required. 2pm

3/28: Actor and author Gianni Russo, *Hollywood Godfather* - 7pm

4/2: Former NY Met Ron Darling, *Loose Threads*. 7 pm

4/4:: Local Author Michael Medico, *Absolutely, Positively, Genuine, Real Fake News*. 7pm

4/11: Local Author Debra M. Roberts, *The Relationship Protocol*. 7pm

4/25: Former right fielder for the '69 Mets Art Shamsky, *After the Miracle*, 7pm

4/28: Former speaker of the house Newt Gingrich, *Collusion*, 7pm

5/7: Local Author C.M Kushins. *Nothing's Bad Luck*. 7pm

....

Please visit www.bookrevue.com
313 New York Ave, Huntington, NY 11743
631-271-1442

13

CATEGORIES

French

Fried Chicken

Gastropub

German

14

16

Japanese/Sushi

18

CATEGORIES

19

20

Small Plates

Soul Food

Southern

22

RESTAURANTS BY
NEIGHBORHOOD

Brooklyn
Al Di La
Applewood
Areo
Blue Ribbon Brasserie
Blue Ribbon Sushi

Bonita
Brooklyn Fish Camp
ChipShop
Convivium Osteria
Defonte's

Di Fara Pizza
Diner
DuMont
Egg
Faicco's
Five Front
Frankies 457 Spuntino
Franny's
Garden Cafe
Ghenet
The Good Fork
The Grocery
Habana Outpost
Hecho en Dumbo
Henry's End
Joe's Pizza
Ki Sushi

La Villa Pizzeria
Locanda Vini & Olii
Lucali
Luz
Noodle Pudding
Peter Luger Steak House
Petite Crevette
Po
Queen Restaurant
Relish
The River Café
Saul
Settepani Bakery
The Smoke Joint
Tanoreen
Tom's Restaurant

Chelsea

Amy's Bread
Billy's Bakery
Cookshop
Da Umberto
Del Posto
La Bergamote

Murray's Bagels
Omai
Patsy's Pizzeria
The Red Cat
Sarabeth's
Tía Pol

Chinatown

Amazing 66
Big Wong
Doyers Vietnamese
Food Sing 88 Corp.
Fuleen Seafood
Joe's Shanghai

Jumbo Hot Dogs
New Bo Ky
Oriental Garden
Orig. Chtwn. Ice Cream
Pho Viet Huong

East Village/NoHo

Angelica Kitchen
Angon on the Sixth
B & H Dairy Restaurant
Back Forty
Cafe Mogador

Caracas Arepa Bar
Degustation
Dessert Truck
Dumpling Man
Hearth

24

Holy Basil
Hummus Place
Mamoun's
Momofuku Noodle Bar
Momofuku Ssäm Bar

Moustache
Prune
Pylos
Veselka
Westville East

Financial District

Adrienne's Pizzabar
Alan's Falafel
Bennie's Thai Cafe
Bread & Olive
Bridge Cafe

Harry's Cafe and Steak
Les Halles
MarkJoseph Steakhouse
Wall Street Burger Shp.
Zaitzeff

Garment District

Gahm Mi Oak
Gray's Papaya
Keens Steakhouse

Lazzara's Pizza Cafe
WonJo

Gramercy/Madison Park

A Voce
Bar Milano
Blue Smoke
Chino's
Eleven Madison Park
Ess-a-Bagel
Les Halles
Novitá

Posto
Resto
Saravanaas
Shake Shack
Tabla/Bread Bar
Tamarind
Turkish Kitchen

Greenwich Village

Aki
Amy's Bread
Annisa
Babbo
Blue Hill
Cru
Gotham Bar and Grill
Gray's Papaya
Hummus Place
Il Mulino
Jane

Joe's Pizza
Lupa
Mamoun's
Mas
Murray's Bagels
Otto
Patsy's Pizzeria
Pearl Oyster Bar
Po
Saigon Grill

Harlem

A Taste of Seafood
Africa Kine
Amy Ruth's
Charles' South-Style Kit.
Dinosaur Bar-B-Que
La Fonda Boricua
Patsy's Pizzeria (original)
Settepani Bakery
Strictly Roots
Zoma

Little Italy/NoLita

Bánh Mì Saigon Bakery
Cafe Colonial
Cafe el Portal
Café Habana
Eight Mile Creek
Epistrophy
Ghenet
Il Cortile
The Kitchen Club
La Esquina
Lovely Day
Peasant
Pinche Taqueria
Public
24 Prince

Lower East Side

Ápizz
Brown Café
Clinton St. Baking Co.
Dumpling House
Falai
Frankies 17 Spuntino
'Inoteca
Katz's Delicatessen
Kuma Inn
Russ & Daughters
Schiller's Liquor Bar
Tides Seafood
wd-50

Midtown East/Murray Hill

Alto
Amma
Aquavit
Artisanal
Avra
BLT Steak
Carl's Steaks
Dawat
Dessert Truck
Ess-a-Bagel
Felidia
The Four Seasons
Hatsuhana
L'Atlr. de Joël Robuchon
La Gioconda
La Grenouille
Murray Hill Diner
Oceana
Pampano
Patsy's Pizzeria
Rosa Mexicano
Sakagura
Sarge's Deli
2nd Ave Deli
Shun Lee Palace
Smith & Wollensky

Sparks Steak House
Sushi Yasuda

Teodora

Midtown West/Theater District

Amy's Bread
Azuri Cafe
Becco
Blue Rib. Sushi Bar/Grill
Bread & Olive
Burger Joint
DB Bistro Moderne
Eatery
Esca
Estiatorio Milos
Insieme
Island Burgers & Shakes
Joe's Shanghai
La Bergamote
Lazzara's Pizza Cafe

Le Bernardin
Masa
The Modern
Molyvos
Norma's
Per Se
Piano Due
Rice 'n' Beans
Sarabeth's
Sugiyama
Sushi of Gari
Sushi Zen
Town
Yakitori Totto

SoHo

27

Alidoro
Aquagrill
Balthazar
Blue Ribbon Brasserie
Blue Ribbon Sushi
Fiamma
Kittichai
L'Ecole

Lucky Strike
Lure Fishbar
Mooncake Foods
Omen
Raoul's
Savoy
Snack
Woo Lae Oak

TriBeCa

Blaue Gans
Bouley
Bouley Upstairs
Bread Tribeca
Carl's Steaks
Chanterelle
Landmarc
Matsugen
Nam

Nobu
Nobu Next Door
Pakistan Tea House
Scalini Fedeli

Union Square/Flatiron

Bar Jamón
Boqueria
Casa Mono
Chat 'n Chew
Craft
Eisenberg's Sandwich Shp.
Fleur de Sel
Giorgio's of Gramercy
Gramercy Tavern
L'Express
Mesa Grill
Old Town Bar & Rest.
Ottimo
Pure Food and Wine
Republic
Rosa Mexicano
71 Irving Place Coffee
Tocqueville
Union Square Cafe
Veritas

Upper East Side

Atlantic Grill
Aureole
Beyoglu
Café Boulud
Candle Cafe/Candle 79
Daniel
davidburke & donatella
Donguri
EJ's Luncheonette
Erminia
Etats-Unis
Ithaka
JoJo
Land Northeast Thai
Paola's
Patsy's Pizzeria
Payard Patisserie & Bist.
Sable's
Sarabeth's
Sette Mezzo
Sushi of Gari
Taco Taco

Upper West Side

Absolute Bagels
Barney Greengrass
Big Nick's
Café des Artistes
Cafe Fiorello
Cafe Luxembourg
Calle Ocho
Celeste
'Cesca
Dovetail
EJ's Luncheonette
Gabriel's Bar & Rest.
Gennaro
Gray's Papaya
Hummus Place
Jean Georges
Land Thai Kitchen
The Neptune Room
Nice Matin
Ouest
Patsy's Pizzeria
Picholine
Rigoletto Pizza
Rosa Mexicano
Saigon Grill
Sarabeth's
Super Tacos
Sushi of Gari
Telepan
Zabar's Cafe

28

NEIGHBORHOODS

West Village/Meatpacking District

A Salt & Battery
A.O.C.
Barbuto
Corner Bistro
Faicco's
The Little Owl
Malatesta Trattoria
Mary's Fish Camp
Merkato 55

Moustache
Pastis
Perry St
Piccolo Angolo
Spice Market
The Spotted Pig
Tartine
Tavern on Jane
Westville

RESTAURANTS BY
PRICE RANGE

$ - Average entrée $10 or less
$$ - Average entrée $11–$25
$$$ - Average entrée $26–$40
$$$$ - Average entrée/prix fixe $41–$70
$$$$$ - Average entrée/prix fixe over $70

29

$ - Average entrée $10 or less

A Salt & Battery
Absolute Bagels
Alan's Falafel
Alidoro
Amy's Bread
B & H Dairy Restaurant
Bánh Mì Saigon Bakery
Big Wong
Billy's Bakery
Burger Joint
Caracas Arepa Bar
Carl's Steaks
Charles' South.-Style Kit.
Corner Bistro
Defonte's
Dessert Truck
Doyers Vietnamese
Dumpling House

Dumpling Man
Eisenberg's Sandwich Shp.
Ess-a-Bagel
Faicco's
Food Sing 88 Corp.
Gray's Papaya
Hummus Place
Island Burgers & Shakes
Joe's Pizza
Jumbo Hot Dogs
La Bergamote
La Esquina (Taqueria)
Lovely Day
Mamoun's
Mooncake Foods
Murray's Bagels
New Bo Ky
Old Town Bar & Rest.

Orig. Chtwn. Ice Cream
Pakistan Tea House
Pinche Taqueria
Russ & Daughters
Sable's
Saravanaas
Settepani Bakery

71 Irving Place Coffee
Shake Shack
Strictly Roots
Super Tacos
Tom's Restaurant
Yakitori Totto
Zabar's Cafe

$$ - Average entrée $11–$25

A Taste of Seafood
Adrienne's Pizzabar
Africa Kine
Al Di La
Amazing 66
Amma
Amy Ruth's
Angelica Kitchen
Angon on the Sixth
A.O.C.
Applewood
Aquavit (café)
Areo
Azuri Cafe
Back Forty
Bar Jamón
Barbuto
Barney Greengrass
Bennie's Thai Cafe
Beyoglu
Big Nick's
Blue Smoke
Bonita
Boqueria
Bread & Olive
Brooklyn Fish Camp
Brown Café
Cafe Colonial
Cafe el Portal
Café Habana/Outpost
Cafe Mogador
Candle Cafe/Candle 79

Celeste
Chat 'n Chew
Chino's
ChipShop
Clinton St. Baking Co.
Convivium Osteria
Dawat
Degustation
Di Fara Pizza
Diner
Dinosaur Bar-B-Que
DuMont
Eatery
Egg
Eight Mile Creek
EJ's Luncheonette
Epistrophy
Five Front
Frankies 17/457 Spuntino
Franny's
Fuleen Seafood
Gahm Mi Oak
Garden Cafe
Gennaro
Ghenet
Giorgio's of Gramercy
The Good Fork
Gramercy Tavern (Tavern)
Hecho en Dumbo
Henry's End
Holy Basil
'Inoteca

30

Ithaka
Jane
Joe's Shanghai
Katz's Delicatessen
Ki Sushi
Kuma Inn
L'Express
La Esquina (Brasserie)
La Fonda Boricua
La Gioconda
La Villa Pizzeria
Land Thai/Land N'east
Lazzara's Pizza Cafe
Les Halles
Lucali
Lucky Strike
Lupa
Luz
Malatesta Trattoria
Mary's Fish Camp
Momofuku Noodle Bar
Momofuku Ssäm Bar
Moustache
Murray Hill Diner
Nam
Nice Matin
Noodle Pudding
Norma's
Novitá
Omai
Oriental Garden
Otto
Patsy's Pizzeria (original)
Patsy's Pizzeria

Petite Crevette
Pho Viet Huong
Po
Posto
Queen Restaurant
The Red Cat
Relish
Republic
Rice 'n' Beans
Rigoletto Pizza
Rosa Mexicano
Saigon Grill
Sakagura
Sarabeth's
Sarge's Deli
Schiller's Liquor Bar
2nd Ave Deli
The Smoke Joint
Snack
Spice Market
Taco Taco
Tanoreen
Tartine
Tavern on Jane
Tía Pol
Tides Seafood
Turkish Kitchen
24 Prince
Veselka
Wall Street Burger Shp.
Westville/Westville East
WonJo
Zaitzeff
Zoma

$$$ - Average entrée $26–$40

A Voce
Aki
Annisa
Ápizz
Aquagrill

Artisanal
Atlantic Grill
Avra
Babbo
Balthazar

Bar Milano
Becco
Blaue Gans
Blue Hill
Blue Ribbon Brasserie
Blue Ribbon Sushi
Bouley Upstairs
Bread Bar at Tabla
Bread Tribeca
Bridge Cafe
Café Boulud
Café des Artistes
Cafe Fiorello
Cafe Luxembourg
Calle Ocho
Casa Mono
'Cesca
Cookshop
Da Umberto
davidburke & donatella
DB Bistro Moderne
Donguri
Dovetail
Erminia
Esca
Etats-Unis
Falai
Felidia
Gabriel's Bar & Rest.
The Grocery
Harry's Cafe and Stk. (cafe)
Hatsuhana
Hearth
Il Cortile
Insieme
JoJo
The Kitchen Club
Kittichai
Landmarc
The Little Owl
Locanda Vini & Olii
Lure Fishbar

Mas
Matsugen
Merkato 55
Mesa Grill
The Modern (Bar Room)
Molyvos
The Neptune Room
Nobu
Nobu Next Door
Omen
Ottimo
Ouest
Pampano
Paola's
Pastis
Payard Patisserie & Bist.
Pearl Oyster Bar
Peasant
Perry St
Piano Due
Piccolo Angolo
Prune
Public
Pure Food and Wine
Pylos
Raoul's
Resto
Saul
Savoy
Sette Mezzo
Shun Lee Palace
The Spotted Pig
Sugiyama
Sushi of Gari
Sushi Yasuda
Sushi Zen
Tamarind
Telepan
Teodora
Tocqueville
Town
Union Square Cafe

A GUIDE TO THE BEST RESTAURANTS

wd-50
Woo Lae Oak

$$$$ - Average entrée/prix fixe $41–$70

Alto	Keens Steakhouse
BLT Steak	L'Atlr. de Joël Robuchon
Bouley	L'Ecole
Craft	La Grenouille
Del Posto	MarkJoseph Steakhouse
Estiatorio Milos	Scalini Fedeli
The Four Seasons	Smith & Wollensky
Gotham Bar and Grill	Sparks Steak House
Harry's Cafe and Stk. (stk house)	Tabla
Il Mulino	

$$$$$ - Average entrée/prix fixe over $70

Aquavit (Dining Room)	Le Bernardin
Aureole	Masa
Chanterelle	The Modern (Dining Room)
Cru	Oceana
Daniel	Per Se
Eleven Madison Park	Peter Luger Steak House
Fiamma	Picholine
Fleur de Sel	The River Café
Gramercy Tavern	Veritas
Jean Georges	

33

★TOP100 TOP 100 RESTAURANTS

NEW YORK CITY

A Salt & Battery	Avra
Al Di La	Babbo
Alto	Balthazar
Amy Ruth's	Bar Milano
Amy's Bread	Barney Greengrass
Angelica Kitchen	Becco
Aquagrill	BLT Steak
Aquavit	Blue Hill
Artisanal	Blue Rib. Sushi/Bar & Grill
Atlantic Grill	Boqueria
Aureole	Bouley

Burger Joint
Café Boulud
Café des Artistes
Cafe Fiorello
Café Habana/Outpost
Cafe Luxembourg
Cafe Mogador
Calle Ocho
Carl's Steaks
'Cesca
Chanterelle
Corner Bistro
Craft
Daniel
Del Posto
Di Fara Pizza
Diner
Eleven Madison Park
Esca
Ess-a-Bagel
Estiatorio Milos
Etats-Unis
Falai
Fiamma
The Four Seasons
Ghenet
Gotham Bar and Grill
Gramercy Tavern
Gray's Papaya
Hatsuhana
Holy Basil
Il Cortile
Il Mulino
Jean Georges
La Gioconda
Lazzara's Pizza Cafe
Le Bernardin
Lupa
Mary's/Brook. Fish Camp
Mesa Grill
The Modern
Molyvos

Momofuku Noodle Bar
Moustache
Nobu
Norma's
Oceana
Ottimo
Otto
Ouest
Pampano
Patsy's Pizzeria (original)
Payard Patis. & Bistro
Per Se
Peter Luger Steak House
Picholine
Prune
Raoul's
The River Café
Rosa Mexicano
Saigon Grill
Sarabeth's
2nd Ave Deli
Sette Mezzo
Shake Shack
Shun Lee Palace
Sparks Steak House
Spice Market
The Spotted Pig
Sushi of Gari
Sushi Yasuda
Tabla/Bread Bar
Town
Turkish Kitchen
Union Square Cafe
Veritas
wd-50
Woo Lae Oak

34

BEST IN CATEGORY

Best African: **Ghenet**
Best Asian Fusion: **Spice Market**
Best Bagels: **Ess-a-Bagel**
Best Bakery: **Amy's Bread**
Best Bistro: **Cafe Luxembourg**
Best Brasserie: **Balthazar**
Best Breakfast: **Norma's**
Best Brunch: **Sarabeth's**
Best Burgers: **Burger Joint at Le Parker Meridien**
Best Cheese Steaks: **Carl's Steaks**
Best Chinese: **Shun Lee Palace**
Best Contemporary: **Union Square Cafe**
Best Continental: **The Four Seasons**
Best Cuban: **Café Habana/Habana Outpost**
Best Deli: **Barney Greengrass**
Best Dessert: **Payard Patisserie & Bistro**
Best Fish and Chips: **A Salt & Battery**
Best French: **Daniel**
Best Greek: **Estiatorio Milos**
Best Hot Dogs: **Gray's Papaya**
Best Hotel Restaurant: **Bar Milano**
Best Irish/British: **The Spotted Pig**
Best Italian: **Babbo**
Best Japanese/Sushi: **Sushi Yasuda**
Best Korean: **Woo Lae Oak**
Best Middle Eastern: **Moustache**
Best Moroccan: **Cafe Mogador**
Best Noodle House: **Momofuku Noodle Bar**
Best Oysters: **Aquagrill**
Best Pizza: **Di Fara Pizza**
Best Scandinavian: **Aquavit**
Best Seafood: **Le Bernardin**
Best Soul Food: **Amy Ruth's**
Best Southwestern: **Mesa Grill**
Best Steak House: **Peter Luger Steak House**
Best Thai: **Holy Basil**
Best Turkish: **Turkish Kitchen**
Best Vegetarian: **Angelica Kitchen**
Best Vietnamese: **Saigon Grill**

 NEIGHBORHOOD MAPS

Manhattan

Brooklyn

Restaurants are listed alphabetically. If you wish to find a restaurant by category, neighborhood or price range, please refer to the Table of Contents at the front of the book. Neighborhood maps are located at the back of the book, along with a complete index of restaurant names.

NEW YORK
NEW YORK

THE BEST RESTAURANTS

NEW YORK CITY **★TOP100** A Salt & Battery

★ **BEST FISH AND CHIPS IN NYC**

112 Greenwich Ave (bet W 12th and 13th Sts)
New York, NY 10011
(212) 691-2713

Neighborhood Map: **West Village/Meatpacking District**
Categories: **Fish and Chips, Irish/British**
Price Range: **$**
www.asaltandbattery.com

A Salt & Battery provides a strong rebuttal to those who
would make British cuisine the butt of culinary jokes. This
tiny British Isles establishment in the West Village cooks up
such a fine fish and chips that Sam Adams himself would be
tempted to swear allegiance to the crown after a bite. And
who could blame him? What could be better than scoring one
of the six or seven counter seats for some lightly battered
fish, a heaping pile of chips (there are no "fries" here, the
menu notes) and a cold pint of Boddingtons? The all-British
staff only adds to the charm. In the mother country, different
regions are known for offering a particular type of fish, but A
Salt & Battery gives diners favorite options from every area:
Haddock, sole, whiting and pollock (a recent substitution for

cod, which has been notably overfished worldwide) all come wrapped in newspaper. Aside from chips, sides include mushy peas and the ubiquitous (in the UK, anyway) Heinz Baked Beans. It's also received much acclaim from both the media and regular junk food junkies for its deep-fried Mars bar. Beer available. Serving lunch and dinner daily.

New York magazine: Critics' Pick
Zagat: 18 food rating (good to very good)
Time Out New York: Critics' Pick

A Taste of Seafood

★ **BEST SEAFOOD IN HARLEM**
59 E 125th St (near Madison Ave)
New York, NY 10035
(212) 831-5584

Neighborhood Map: **Harlem**
Categories: **Fried Chicken, Seafood, Soul Food**
Price Range: **$$**
www.atasteofseafood.com

Take your place in line to get one of these famed whiting sandwiches. No alcohol available. Serving breakfast, lunch and dinner daily. Closes 6 pm Sun.

A Voce

★ **BEST ITALIAN IN GRAMERCY/MADISON PARK**
41 Madison Ave (near 26th St)
New York, NY 10010
(212) 545-8555

Neighborhood Map: **Gramercy/Madison Park**
Categories: **Contemporary, Italian**
Price Range: **$$$**
www.avocerestaurant.com

Contemporary interpretations of Italian classics are accompanied by an extensive wine list of full and half bottles with offerings from Italy, France and the United States. Reservations suggested. Full bar. Serving lunch Mon–Fri, dinner nightly.

The New York Times: ★★★ (excellent)

38

New York magazine: ★★ (very good); Critics' Pick
Zagat: 25 food rating (very good to excellent)
The Village Voice: Critics' Pick

Absolute Bagels

★ **BEST BAGELS ON THE UPPER WEST SIDE**
2788 Broadway (bet 107th and 108th Sts)
New York, NY 10025
(212) 932-2052

Neighborhood Map: **Upper West Side**
Categories: **Bagels, Breakfast**
Price Range: **$**

Home to one of the Upper West Side's favorite bagels,
Absolute Bagels serves to a constant stream of Columbia
students and others in the neighborhood. Cash only. Serving
breakfast, lunch and dinner daily.

Adrienne's Pizzabar

54 Stone St (near Broad St)
New York, NY 10004
(212) 248-3838

Neighborhood Map: **Financial District**
Categories: **Italian, Pizza**
Price Range: **$$**
www.adriennespizzabar.com

A solid choice for some sit-down pizza in Lower
Manhattan. Full bar. Serving lunch and dinner daily, late-night
Mon–Sat.

The New York Times: Top Pick
New York magazine: ★★ (very good); Critics' Pick
Zagat: 24 food rating (very good to excellent)

Africa Kine

256 W 116th St (near Frederick Douglass Blvd)
New York, NY 10026
(212) 666-9400

39

Neighborhood Map: **Harlem**
Category: **African**
Price Range: **$$**
www.africakine.com

This sumptuous second-story dining room is home to some of the best Senegalese food in the city. No alcohol available. Serving lunch, dinner and late-night daily.

New York magazine: Critics' Pick

Aki

★ **BEST JAPANESE/SUSHI IN GREENWICH VILLAGE**
181 W 4th St (near Jones St)
New York, NY 10014
(212) 989-5440

Neighborhood Map: **Greenwich Village**
Category: **Japanese/Sushi**
Price Range: **$$$**

Chef Siggy Nakanishi, a one-time personal chef in Kingston, Jamaica, infuses the flavors of the Caribbean into inventive Japanese dishes and sushi rolls at this Greenwich Village favorite. Reservations suggested. Beer, wine and sake available. Serving dinner Tue–Sun. Closed Mon.

Zagat: 26 food rating (extraordinary to perfection)

NEW YORK CITY ★**TOP100** Al Di La

★ **BEST ITALIAN IN BROOKLYN**
248 5th Ave (near Carroll St)
Brooklyn, NY 11215
(718) 783-4565

Neighborhood Map: **Brooklyn (Park Slope)**
Category: **Italian**
Price Range: **$$**
www.aldilatrattoria.com

A no-reservations policy and creative, affordable Venetian-inspired fare ensure lines of locals at Park Slope's Al Di La. Not to worry, though: You can grab a seat at the wine bar

40

next door (Al Di La Vino) until your table is ready. Owned by husband-and-wife team Anna Klinger (chef) and Emiliano Coppa, this funky yet subtly romantic trattoria nails the neighborhood feel and is a refreshing respite from the overdone preciousness at Manhattan's most expensive northern Italian restaurants. Steamed Prince Edward Island mussels or grilled sardines over arugula and tripe stewed with white wine, herbs and tomatoes lead off the antipasti. Rustic pastas include the tagliatelle with meat ragu, risotto with cuttlefish, and ravioli stuffed with fava beans, pecorino and mascarpone cheeses. Pork loin scaloppini and the signature braised rabbit with olives and polenta satiate those craving meat. A smooth gelato finish reminds that with Italian cuisine, simplicity can be bliss. Reservations not accepted. Beer and wine available. Serving dinner Wed–Mon. Closed Tue.

The New York Times: ★★ (very good); Top Pick
New York magazine: ★ (good); Critics' Pick
Zagat: 26 food rating (extraordinary to perfection)
Time Out New York: Critics' Pick
The Village Voice: Critics' Pick

41

Alan's Falafel (food cart)

Cedar St at Broadway
New York, NY 10006
(646) 301-2316

Neighborhood Map: **Financial District**
Categories: **Food Cart, Middle Eastern**
Price Range: **$**

A fast-moving line forms at this Liberty Plaza Park pushcart dishing out the latest in mobile Middle Eastern snacks. No alcohol available. Serving during breakfast and lunch hours Mon–Fri. Closed Sat–Sun.

New York magazine: Critics' Pick

Alidoro

★ **BEST SANDWICHES IN SOHO**
105 Sullivan St (near Spring St)
New York, NY 10012
(212) 334-5179

Neighborhood Map: **SoHo**
Categories: **Italian, Sandwiches**
Price Range: **$**

So many sandwiches and so little time. Eat in or take them out — either way, these fresh-made Italian sandwiches are some of the best of their kind. No alcohol available. Serving lunch and early dinner Mon–Sat. Closed Sun.

New York magazine: Critics' Pick

NEW YORK CITY
★TOP 100 Alto

★ **BEST ITALIAN IN MIDTOWN EAST/MURRAY HILL**
11 E 53rd St (bet Madison and 5th Aves)
New York, NY 10022
(212) 308-1099

Neighborhood Map: **Midtown East/Murray Hill**
Category: **Italian**
Price Range: **$$$$**
www.altorestaurant.com

Wine buffs sing the praises of Alto, which boasts some 2,500 vintages and recently received *Wine Spectator*'s much-coveted Grand Award (an addition to its many other distinctions). In a game of musical chefs, star chef Scott Conant left Alto and sister restaurant L'Impero in 2007, but Alto has not missed a note since well-seasoned chef/partner Michael White (formerly of Fiamma) took the reins. This swanky Midtown spot is slightly hidden: Just look for the graffiti-tagged chunk of the Berlin Wall outside. Make your way down to the windowless, mirror- and curtain-clad dining room, with white tablecloths, plush red chairs and walls covered in wine bottles. Service is reputably attentive, and the noise level is refreshingly low. Northern Italian cuisine gets haute treatment and displays some influence from Italy's neighbors to the north. White's menu may include the likes of seafood risotto, pan-seared octopus in a tomato vinaigrette, and orecchiette with cuttlefish, pork sausage and broccoli rabe. Amish veal chop and roasted squab may round out the menu, which offers a four-course, prix fixe option. Jacket suggested. Reservations suggested. Full bar. Serving lunch Mon–Fri, dinner Mon–Sat. Closed Sun.

Michelin Guide: ★ (a very good restaurant in its category)
The New York Times: ★★★ (excellent); Top Pick

New York magazine: ★★ (very good); Critics' Pick
Zagat: 25 food rating (very good to excellent)
The Village Voice: Critics' Pick

Amazing 66

66 Mott St (near Bayard St)
New York, NY 10013
(212) 334-0099

Neighborhood Map: **Chinatown**
Category: **Chinese**
Price Range: **$$**

Here you'll find affordable and family-friendly Cantonese. Beer and wine available. Serving lunch and dinner daily.

Zagat: 23 food rating (very good to excellent)

Amma

★ **BEST INDIAN IN MIDTOWN EAST/MURRAY HILL**

246 E 51st St (near 2nd Ave)
New York, NY 10022
(212) 644-8330

43

Neighborhood Map: **Midtown East/Murray Hill**
Category: **Indian**
Price Range: **$$**
www.ammanyc.com

Amma offers reasonably priced Indian cuisine in a comfortable, homey space and features both a traditional entrée menu as well as a seven-course tasting menu with optional wine pairing. A vegetarian tasting menu is also available. Reservations suggested. Full bar. Serving lunch and dinner daily.

The New York Times: ★★ (very good); Top Pick
New York magazine: Critics' Pick
Zagat: 24 food rating (very good to excellent)

NEW YORK CITY ★**TOP100** Amy Ruth's

★ **BEST SOUL FOOD IN NYC**

113 W 116th St (bet Lenox and 7th Aves)
New York, NY 10026
(212) 280-8779

Neighborhood Map: **Harlem**
Categories: **Soul Food, Southern**
Price Range: **$$**
www.amyruthsharlem.com

Amy Ruth's, named for the grandmother of founder/former
owner Carl Redding, has been putting the "art" in "heart
attack" since 1998 with its perfect renditions of mouth-
watering Southern favorites. Mac and cheese, fall-off-
the-bone ribs, and chicken and waffles (called The Rev. Al
Sharpton on the menu here) attract long lines of soul food
lovers, tourists and late-night diners looking to satisfy
their south-of-the-Mason-Dixon flavor voids. The "waffle
menu" even pairs waffles with more unorthodox items
such as The Dougie Fresh (waffles and fried whiting)
and The Larry Dais (waffles and rib eye). Turkey meat
loaf, chicken and dumplings, and other specials rotate
daily while collard greens, string beans and buttered
corn accompany any meal nicely. A slice of pineapple
coconut cake will ensure another visit in the near future.
No alcohol available. BYOB. Serving breakfast, lunch and
dinner daily. Open 24 hours Fri–Sat.

The New York Times: Top Pick
New York magazine: Critics' Pick
Zagat: 21 food rating (very good to excellent)
Time Out New York: Critics' Pick

★TOP100 Amy's Bread

★ **BEST BAKERY IN NYC**
Neighborhood Map: **Chelsea**
75 9th Ave (bet 15th and 16th Sts)
New York, NY 10011
(212) 462-4338

Neighborhood Map: **Greenwich Village**
250 Bleecker St (near Leroy St)
New York, NY 10014
(212) 675-7802

Neighborhood Map: **Midtown West/Theater District**

44

672 9th Ave (bet 46th and 47th Sts)
New York, NY 10036
(212) 977-2670

Categories: **Bakery, Café, Sandwiches**
Price Range: **$**
www.amysbread.com

Be it bun, loaf or baguette, sourdough, focaccia or
pumpernickel, Amy Scherber has made many a New
Yorker's six to 11 servings a day all the more enjoyable
since opening her Hell's Kitchen shop in 1992 with just five
employees. Now with two additional retail stores (Chelsea
Market and Greenwich Village), a staff of over 100, and
more than 200 wholesale deliveries daily, her citywide
operation is much more equipped to fill the demand for
such delights as prosciutto and black pepper bread, raisin
walnut, or semolina with raisins and fennel. In addition to
whole-grain goodness, Amy's offers an array of excellent
sandwiches, decadent pastries and some of the city's best
cupcakes. No alcohol available. Serving during breakfast,
lunch and dinner hours daily. Check individual stores for
specific hours.

Zagat: 23 food rating (very good to excellent)

NEW YORK CITY
★TOP100 Angelica Kitchen

★ **BEST VEGETARIAN IN NYC**
300 E 12th St (bet 1st and 2nd Aves)
New York, NY 10003
(212) 228-2909

Neighborhood Map: **East Village/NoHo**
Category: **Vegetarian**
Price Range: **$$**
www.angelicakitchen.com

This East Village staple has dished out healthy, exclusively
vegan fare since 1976, before its average patron was in
biodegradable diapers eating organic soy Gerber. Angelica
Kitchen is a restaurant with a clear mission: to use
seasonally sustainable ingredients supplied directly from
farmers and artisans whenever possible. In fact, 95 percent
of the food used to create the menu is grown ecologically. A
sense of community pervades the dining room, as communal

tables encourage eating with strangers. Locals line up out the door for tempeh reuben sandwiches and the signature Dragon Bowls, consisting of rice, beans, tofu, sea vegetables and steamed vegetables. A variety of seasonal soups, salads and spreads are available as well. And be sure to check the specials. As if the bounty of health-conscious vegan options were not enough reason to come, it's also BYOB. Reservations not accepted. No alcohol available. Cash only. Serving lunch and dinner daily.

Zagat: 20 food rating (very good to excellent)
Time Out New York: Critics' Pick

Angon on the Sixth

★ **BEST INDIAN IN THE EAST VILLAGE/NOHO**

320 E 6th St (bet 1st and 2nd Aves)
New York, NY 10003
(212) 260-8229

Neighborhood Map: **East Village/NoHo**
Category: **Indian**
Price Range: **$$**
www.angon.biz

More refined than the average Curry Row eatery, Angon provides excellent renditions of Indian classics in a darkly lit room with paper lanterns and exposed brick walls. Beer and wine available. Serving lunch Tue–Sun, dinner nightly, late-night Fri–Sun.

The New York Times: Top Pick

Annisa

13 Barrow St (bet 7th Ave and W 4th St)
New York, NY 10014
(212) 741-6699

Neighborhood Map: **Greenwich Village**
Category: **Contemporary**
Price Range: **$$$**
www.annisarestaurant.com

Beautiful and elegant Annisa charms diners with its exquisitely prepared contemporary dishes and simple,

46

graceful dining room. Reservations suggested. Full bar.
Serving dinner nightly.

Michelin Guide: ★ (a very good restaurant in its category)
The New York Times: ★★ (very good); Top Pick
New York magazine: ★★★ (generally excellent); Critics' Pick
Zagat: 27 food rating (extraordinary to perfection)
Time Out New York: Critics' Pick

A.O.C.

314 Bleecker St (near Grove St)
New York, NY 10014
(212) 675-9463

Neighborhood Map: **West Village/Meatpacking District**
Categories: **Breakfast, French**
Price Range: **$$**
www.aocnyc.com

Serving breakfast, lunch and dinner, A.O.C. is a favorite spot
for casual French cuisine. The back patio is a delightful find
during warmer months. Full bar. Serving breakfast, lunch,
dinner and late-night daily.

Zagat: 19 food rating (good to very good)

Ápizz

217 Eldridge St (near Stanton St)
New York, NY 10002
(212) 253-9199

Neighborhood Map: **Lower East Side**
Categories: **Italian, Pizza**
Price Range: **$$$**
www.apizz.com

From the restaurateurs who brought you Peasant comes this
darkly lit, cozy dining room on the Lower East Side, known
for its brick-oven pizzas and a nice wine list. Reservations
suggested. Full bar. Serving dinner nightly.

New York magazine: Critics' Pick
Zagat: 24 food rating (very good to excellent)

Applewood

501 11th St (near 7th Ave)
Brooklyn, NY 11215
(718) 788-1014

Neighborhood Map: **Brooklyn (Park Slope)**
Categories: **Brunch, Contemporary, Small Plates**
Price Range: **$$**
www.applewoodny.com

Park Slopers and Manhattanites adore Applewood, with its
comfortable cottage-like interior, for its daily changing menus
filled with locally sourced ingredients and consistent
creativity. Reservations suggested. Full bar. Serving dinner
Tue–Sat. Sun brunch 10 am–3 pm.

The New York Times: Top Pick
New York magazine: ★★ (very good); Critics' Pick
Zagat: 25 food rating (very good to excellent)

NEW YORK CITY
★TOP100 Aquagrill

★ BEST OYSTERS IN NYC
210 Spring St (near 6th Ave)
New York, NY 10012
(212) 274-0505

Neighborhood Map: **SoHo**
Categories: **Brunch, Oysters, Seafood**
Price Range: **$$$**
www.aquagrill.com

Jonathan Swift once mused, "He was a bold man that first ate
an oyster," but at Aquagrill, it doesn't take an act of courage
to dive into the 25–30 varieties of oysters served daily, as
all the oceanic offerings here are fresh and exquisitely
prepared. Husband-and-wife team Jeremy (chef) and Jennifer
(sommelier) Marshall's unfussy SoHo hotspot draws rave
reviews for its seafood specialties, desserts made in-house
and weekend brunch at reasonable prices. Aside from the
famed raw bar, which has served more than 200 varieties
of oysters since Aquagrill opened in 1996, seafood delights
include falafel-crusted salmon, bouillabaisse, and seared
diver scallops with Dungeness crabmeat risotto. For dessert,
there's roasted caramelized grapefruit with grapefruit sorbet

or the warm apple tart with cinnamon ice cream and caramel sauce. Reservations suggested. Full bar. Serving lunch Mon–Fri, dinner nightly. Sat–Sun brunch noon–3:45 pm.

The New York Times: ★★ (very good)
New York magazine: Critics' Pick
Zagat: 26 food rating (extraordinary to perfection)
Time Out New York: Critics' Pick

NEW YORK CITY
★TOP100 Aquavit

★ **BEST SCANDINAVIAN IN NYC**
65 E 55th St (near Madison Ave)
New York, NY 10022
(212) 307-7311

Neighborhood Map: **Midtown East/Murray Hill**
Categories: **Brunch, Contemporary, Scandinavian**
Price Range: **Dining Room $$$$$ Café $$**
www.aquavit.org

49

Perennial favorite Aquavit moved down the street from its waterfall-bedecked digs to the Park Avenue Tower on 55th Street in 2005. The minimalist, space-agey new venue is full of Scandinavian chic. Swedish chef Marcus Samuelsson won the James Beard Foundation's 2003 Best Chef: New York award, and he continues to astound locals and critics alike with his modern Nordic cuisine. Snag a spot on an "Egg Chair" or "Swan Sofa" in the bar and lounge, and take a bracing shot of the liquor for which the restaurant is named — there are numerous flavors, in addition to aquavit cocktails. The prix fixe dinner and the chef's tasting choices (with optional wine pairings) constitute the menu. Signature appetizers such as the herring sampler and the foie gras ganache headline, while second-course favorites include hot-smoked trout and the seared rib eye with red onion marmalade and oxtail. Or, if you're short on time, stomach capacity or appropriate attire for the prix fixe main dining room, stop in the café for Swedish meatballs, steamed mussels, herring à la carte or the chef's Smorgasbord, an "assortment of Swedish bites." Jacket suggested for dining room. Reservations suggested. Full bar. Dining room serving lunch Mon–Fri, dinner nightly. Sun brunch noon–2:30 pm. Café serving lunch Mon–Sat, dinner nightly.

The New York Times: ★★★ (excellent); Top Pick
New York magazine: ★★★★ (exceptional; consistently elite);
   Critics' Pick
Zagat: 25 food rating (very good to excellent)
Time Out New York: Critics' Pick

Areo

8424 3rd Ave (near 85th St)
Brooklyn, NY 11209
(718) 238-0079

Neighborhood Map: **Brooklyn (Bay Ridge)**
Category: **Italian**
Price Range: **$$**

This 20-year-old trattoria in Bay Ridge doles out plentiful
portions of upscale Italian in a lively, consistently packed
dining room. Full bar. Serving lunch and dinner daily.

Zagat: 25 food rating (very good to excellent)

NEW YORK CITY
★TOP100 Artisanal

★ **BEST BISTRO IN MIDTOWN EAST/MURRAY HILL**
2 Park Ave (ent on 32nd St)
New York, NY 10016
(212) 725-8585

Neighborhood Map: **Midtown East/Murray Hill**
Categories: **Bistro, Brunch, French**
Price Range: **$$$**
www.artisanalbistro.com

Blessed are the cheesemakers indeed. Boasting more than
250 varieties from which to choose, Artisanal is veritable
holy ground for cheese enthusiasts. With multiple fondues,
charcuterie and fromage samplings for the whole table, and
every wine available by the glass, Artisanal inspires decadent
dining. Beyond the cheese — yes, it's difficult to get beyond
the cheese, but try — Artisanal offers both classic and
creative renditions of French bistro fare with onion soup,
hanger steak frites (made with filet) and sautéed skate wing
with a blood orange Grenobloise. Bouillabaisse and steak au
poivre are among rotating daily specials. And all of this can

be enjoyed in a chic art deco dining room reminiscent of a Parisian bistro. For dessert, there's chocolate fondue for two or the apple tart Tatin with a cheddar cheese crust. If you've overindulged, you can choose any number of selections from the "cheese cave" to take home. Full bar with extensive wine list. Serving lunch Mon–Fri, dinner nightly. Late-night Fri–Sat. Sat–Sun brunch 11 am–5 pm.

The New York Times: ★★ (very good); Top Pick
New York magazine: ★★ (very good); Critics' Pick
Zagat: 23 food rating (very good to excellent)
Time Out New York: Critics' Pick
The Village Voice: Critics' Pick

NEW YORK CITY
★TOP100 Atlantic Grill

★ BEST SEAFOOD ON THE UPPER EAST SIDE
1341 3rd Ave (near 77th St)
New York, NY 10021
(212) 988-9200

Neighborhood Map: **Upper East Side**
Categories: **Brunch, Japanese/Sushi, Oysters, Seafood**
Price Range: **$$$**
www.brguestrestaurants.com

51

When a weekend getaway to the Cape isn't an option, the Upper East Side flocks to restaurant mogul Steve Hanson's (Blue Fin, Blue Water Grill, Ruby Foo's) chic Atlantic Grill, a stalwart for reliable ocean bounty since setting sail in 1998. The wicker chairs evoke a posh beach-club chill in the bar area, where the regulars sip gin and tonics and down oysters on the half shell. With a Pan-Asian sushi bar, a lobster pot and a wood-burning grill at the keel, the kitchen keeps things interesting without navigating into unfamiliar waters. More adventurous diners spring for the likes of nori-wrapped bigeye tuna, horseradish-crusted salmon with roasted Georgia peaches, and the crispy coconut lobster roll with papaya and sake-mustard sauce, while a nightly selection of "simply grilled" fish and remarkably fresh raw selections keep those longing for *au naturel* fully satisfied. Either way, dessert is a must. *Wine Spectator* award-winning wine list. Full bar. Serving lunch Mon–Sat, dinner nightly. Late-night Thu–Sat. Sun brunch 10:30 am–4pm.

The New York Times: ★ (good); Top Pick
Zagat: 23 food rating (very good to excellent)

Aureole

★ **BEST CONTEMPORARY ON THE UPPER EAST SIDE**

34 E 61st St (bet Madison and Park Aves)
New York, NY 10021
(212) 319-1660

Neighborhood Map: **Upper East Side**
Category: **Contemporary**
Price Range: **$$$$$**
www.charliepalmer.com

This brownstone on the Upper East Side, once home to
Orson Welles, remains one of New York's most elegant and
celebrated restaurants. Owner Charlie Palmer, who graduated
from the Culinary Institute of America and opened Aureole at
the young age of 28, has written four cookbooks, won a James
Beard award for Best Chef: New York, and has expanded his
business to include multiple restaurants and hotels across
the country. (He no longer cooks here.) The two floors of
dining space have special occasion written all over them
while remaining grounded and unfussy. Starters on executive
chef Tony Aiazzi's seasonal prix fixe menu may include the
likes of three-cheese ravioli or the charcuterie selection,
which includes house-made terrines and sausages. Entrées
feature creative, contemporary renditions of fine-dining
classics such as butter-roasted Maine lobster and thyme-
roasted beef filet with black pepper and horseradish gnocchi.
Impressively, there's also an entire vegetarian tasting menu.
Skipping dessert should not be considered, with finishing
touches such as maple and sweet corn flan and caramelized
mission fig upside-down cake. Reservations required. Full bar
with extensive, renowned wine list. Serving dinner Mon–Sat.
Closed Sun.

Michelin Guide: ★ (a very good restaurant in its category)
The New York Times: ★★ (very good); Top Pick
New York magazine: Critics' Pick
Zagat: 27 food rating (extraordinary to perfection)

Avra

141 E 48th St (bet Lexington and 3rd Aves)
New York, NY 10017
(212) 759-8550

Neighborhood Map: **Midtown East/Murray Hill**
Categories: **Brunch, Greek, Oysters, Seafood**
Price Range: **$$$**
www.avrany.com

No need to make that down payment on a villa in the Greek Isles. Avra's breezy atmosphere and the smell of freshly grilled fish will whisk you away for much cheaper. Homey would be an appropriate description, and the restaurant itself claims to replicate "a cozy space evocative of an Ionian home," with white walls, blue ceilings, an open kitchen and decorative tables covered with ceramics and vegetables. Avra lets the sea speak for itself with simple preparations of raw bar favorites and grilled fish. Appetizers receiving the Greek treatment include spanakopita with sea bass and Prince Edward Island mussels steamed with feta, ouzo (a Greek liqueur), fresh tomato and herbs. Whole fish is priced by the pound and grilled over charcoal. New Zealand snapper, Maine lobster, Dover sole and Mediterranean white snapper are among possible offerings. Reservations required. Full bar. Serving lunch Mon–Fri, dinner nightly. Late-night Mon–Sat. Sat–Sun brunch 11 am–4 pm.

The New York Times: ★ (good)
New York magazine: Critics' Pick
Zagat: 24 food rating (very good to excellent)
Time Out New York: Critics' Pick

53

Azuri Cafe

★ BEST MIDDLE EASTERN IN MIDTOWN WEST/THEATER DISTRICT

465 W 51st St (bet 9th and 10th Aves)
New York, NY 10019
(212) 262-2920

Neighborhood Map: **Midtown West/Theater District**
Categories: **Kosher, Middle Eastern**
Price Range: **$$**

Tasty kosher eats are the name of the game at this Hell's Kitchen hole in the wall owned by a husband-and-wife team of native Israelis whose own website concedes Azuri Cafe "is not the most stylish place around. It's not the friendliest either." No alcohol available. Serving lunch Sun–Fri, dinner Sun–Thu. Closed Sat.

The New York Times: Top Pick
Zagat: 25 food rating (very good to excellent)

B & H Dairy Restaurant
127 2nd Ave (bet 7th St and St. Marks Pl)
New York, NY 10003
(212) 505-8065

Neighborhood Map: **East Village/NoHo**
Categories: **Breakfast, Kosher, Vegetarian**
Price Range: **$**

If you're homesick for old New York, visit this tiny, old-school lunch counter with vegetarian and kosher specialties, including some of the best blintzes in the city. No alcohol available. Serving breakfast, lunch and dinner daily.

The Village Voice: Critics' Pick

★TOP100 Babbo
NEW YORK CITY

★ **BEST ITALIAN IN NYC**
110 Waverly Pl (bet Washington Sq Park and 6th Ave)
New York, NY 10011
(212) 777-0303

Neighborhood Map: **Greenwich Village**
Category: **Italian**
Price Range: **$$$**
www.babbonyc.com

White-hot since its 1998 opening, Babbo Ristorante e Enoteca possesses 90 of the most foodie-coveted seats in the city. That is, at least in part, due to chef/co-owner Mario Batali's national reputation as emperor of the restaurateuring world. Though he owns interest in ventures from New York's Esca, Lupa and Del Posto to Los Angeles' — and perhaps the country's — toughest reservation, Osteria Mozza, Batali still sets his throne inside the kitchen of his Greenwich Village pet, jamming to his iPod (which plays throughout the dining room) and preparing his most intensely flavored menu of all. From goose liver ravioli to lamb's tongue salad, His Highness brings new meaning to haute cuisine, preparing flawless pastas and succulent meat dishes as he imagines an Italian in the Hudson Valley would. Reservations

---

suggested. Full bar. Serving dinner nightly.

The New York Times: ★★★ (excellent); Top Pick
New York magazine: ★★★★ (exceptional; consistently elite);
    Critics' Pick
Zagat: 27 food rating (extraordinary to perfection)
Time Out New York: Critics' Pick

Back Forty

190 Ave B (near 12th St)
New York, NY 10009
(212) 388-1990

Neighborhood Map: **East Village/NoHo**
Categories: **Brunch**, **Contemporary**
Price Range: **$$**
www.backfortynyc.com

Gayot.com calls locavore chef Peter Hoffman's friendly and
casual neighborhood eatery "a Greenmarket paradise on
Avenue B." A grass-fed burger and a basket of fries with
rosemary sea salt really hit the spot. Full bar. Serving dinner
nightly, late-night Fri–Sat. Sun brunch noon–3:30 pm.

Zagat: 19 food rating (good to very good)

55

NEW YORK CITY **★TOP100** Balthazar

★ **BEST BRASSERIE IN NYC**
80 Spring St (near Crosby St)
New York, NY 10012
(212) 965-1785

Neighborhood Map: **SoHo**
Categories: **Brasserie, Breakfast, Brunch, French,
    Oysters**
Price Range: **$$$**
www.balthazarny.com

Voulez vous manger avec moi çe soir? Yes? Well then, let's
go to Balthazar, where the dining room's beautiful dark
woods, smallish tables and French menu require only a dash
of imagination to feel transported to a Parisian brasserie.
Beyond a healthy selection of traditional entrées such as

duck confit with crispy potatoes, wild mushrooms and frisée salad, and seared organic salmon with corn, leeks and chanterelles, Balthazar also has an extensive wine menu and a raw seafood bar offering "fruit of the sea": oysters, littleneck clams, crab and lobster. While the likes of *New York* magazine have hailed the restaurant, which opened in 1997, as nothing short of "an evocation of a Paris brasserie that outglows anything within Brie-tossing distance of the Seine," be advised that its popularity has spawned a bit of a table-cramping momentum that may yield confining leg space or too much information overheard from the next table. And so it's convenient that the adjacent Balthazar bakery offers delicious breads, pastries, soups, sandwiches and salads to go. Berets and pointy shoes optional, but reservations recommended. Full bar. Serving breakfast, lunch and late-night daily. Sat–Sun brunch 10 am–4 pm.

The New York Times: ★★ (very good); Top Pick
New York magazine: ★★★ (generally excellent); Critics' Pick
Zagat: 23 food rating (very good to excellent)
Time Out New York: Critics' Pick

Bánh Mì Saigon Bakery

★ BEST SANDWICHES IN LITTLE ITALY/NOLITA

138 Mott St (near Grand St)
New York, NY 10002
(212) 941-1541

Neighborhood Map: **Little Italy/NoLita**
Categories: **Sandwiches, Vietnamese**
Price Range: **$**

I scream. You scream. We all scream for bánh mì! Tender roast pork, pickled vegetables and a fresh baguette at this tiny Little Italy sandwich shop comprise a hefty, cheap sandwich that is definitely worth shouting about. No alcohol available. Cash only. Serving lunch and early dinner Tue–Sun. Closed Mon.

The Village Voice: Critics' Pick

Bar Jamón

125 E 17th St (near Irving Pl)
New York, NY 10003
(212) 253-2773

Neighborhood Map: **Union Square/Flatiron**
Categories: **Small Plates, Spanish**
Price Range: **$$**
www.barjamonnyc.com

A touch more casual (and keeping later hours) than big brother Casa Mono around the corner, this tiny tapas bar, brought to you by Mario Batali and Joseph Bastianich, has a 600-bottle wine list and serves up cured meats, specialty cheeses and various other bite-sized Spanish delicacies. Beer and wine available. Serving lunch, dinner and late-night daily.

Time Out New York: Critics' Pick

NEW YORK CITY
★TOP100 **Bar Milano**

★ **BEST HOTEL RESTAURANT IN NYC**
323 3rd Ave (near 24th St, Hotel Marcel)
New York, NY 10010
(212) 683-3035

Neighborhood Map: **Gramercy/Madison Park**
Categories: **Brunch, Contemporary, Hotel Restaurant, Italian**
Price Range: **$$$**
www.barmilano.com

Bar Milano (from the people who brought you Inoteca, Ino and Lupa) makes itself available to high rollers and impulsive spenders well into the late-night hours. But you can also start your Saturday at the bustling bar area for brunch, with lobster and eggs and a Luce Del Sole (grapefruit vodka, honey syrup, and freshly squeezed lemon and orange juices). Starkly contrasting the Denton brothers' more casual Italian endeavors, this cavernous Gramercy dining spot is refined and swanky, with leather booths, high ceilings and marble slabs covering the walls. As to be expected by the name of the place, the fare is largely ambitious and elevated northern Italian. Braised tripe polenta, osso buco veal agnolotti and rabbit *fazzoletti* occupy the primi portion of the menu. The meats and seafood of the secondi section have drawn more praise, however, from veal Milanese covered in breadcrumbs to scallops with caviar, sunchokes and shallots. A number of gelatos, sorbets and cheeses are available for dessert. Reservations suggested. Full bar with extensive wine list and innovative cocktails. Serving lunch, dinner and late-night daily. Sat–Sun brunch 10 am–3:30 pm.

The New York Times: ★★ (very good)
New York magazine: ★★ (very good); Critics' Pick
Zagat: 22 food rating (very good to excellent)

Barbuto
775 Washington St (near W 12th St)
New York, NY 10014
(212) 924-9700

Neighborhood Map: **West Village/Meatpacking District**
Category: **Italian**
Price Range: **$$**
www.barbutonyc.com

Seasoned chef Jonathan Waxman's latest venture, Barbuto, comes complete with retractable garage doors for sidewalk dining. This casual bistro features affordable and seasonally changing Italian-inspired fare, not to mention the chef's signature roasted chicken. Reservations suggested. Full bar. Serving lunch and dinner daily, late-night Thu–Sat.

The New York Times: ★ (good)
New York magazine: ★ (good); Critics' Pick
Zagat: 21 food rating (very good to excellent)
Time Out New York: Critics' Pick

 **Barney Greengrass**

★ **BEST DELI IN NYC**
541 Amsterdam Ave (near 86th St)
New York, NY 10024
(212) 724-4707

Neighborhood Map: **Upper West Side**
Categories: **Bagels, Breakfast, Brunch, Deli**
Price Range: **$$**
www.barneygreengrass.com

Stand in the notoriously lengthy line, browse the Sunday *Times* at your charmingly minute table, and be a part of New York at

Barney Greengrass, where the lox is delectably salty and bagels without holes (aka bialys) still exist. Since opening in Harlem in 1908 and moving to the Upper West Side, this family-run institution has brought a century of excellence to Manhattan's borscht-and-latke-loving noshers. Fish for breakfast has never seemed so right as in one of Barney's trademark scrambles — featuring Nova Scotia salmon, sturgeon or lox scrambled with eggs and onions — but you'll also get your pretty penny's worth with a simple bagel and cream cheese. Beer available. Cash only. Serving breakfast and lunch Tue–Sun (until 4 pm Tue–Fri, 5 pm Sat–Sun). Closed Mon.

The New York Times: Top Pick
New York magazine: Critics' Pick
Zagat: 24 food rating (very good to excellent)
The Village Voice: Critics' Pick

***

NEW YORK CITY **★TOP100** **Becco**

355 W 46th St (bet 8th and 9th Aves)
New York, NY 10036
(212) 397-7597

59

Neighborhood Map: **Midtown West/Theater District**
Category: **Italian**
Price Range: **$$$**
www.becco-nyc.com

Though you wouldn't expect "celebrity chef" and "all-you-can-eat" to pertain to the same New York restaurant, the descriptions fit the bill for this pre-theater favorite on Restaurant Row. PBS persona/cookbook author/nationwide restaurateur Lidia Bastianich and her son Joseph opened this brightly colored town house trattoria in 1993. A unique prix fixe features three specialty pasta dishes (which change daily) that are freshly made and delivered tableside. Throw in a choice of antipasti or a classic Caesar salad, with plenty of fine Italian wine to boot, and this gourmet meal is a steal. Executive chef William Gallagher excels with à la carte options as well, ranging from the signature osso buco to a grilled whole fish of the day or pork scallopini stuffed with pancetta, pistachio and bread crumbs. After such a filling meal, it'd probably be better to attend an Ibsen or Chekhov drama rather than a gut-busting Monty Python or Mel Brooks adaptation. Note: Chef Gallagher has cooked for the Pope on his visit to New York

City. If it's good enough for His Holiness, then it's good enough for you. Full bar. Serving lunch and dinner daily. Late-night Tue–Sat.

The New York Times: Top Pick
Zagat: 23 food rating (very good to excellent)

Bennie's Thai Cafe

★ **BEST THAI IN THE FINANCIAL DISTRICT**

88 Fulton St (bet Gold and William Sts)
New York, NY 10038
(212) 587-8930

Neighborhood Map: **Financial District**
Category: **Thai**
Price Range: **$$**

Quick service and low prices make this a haven for Thai food lovers in Lower Manhattan. Beer and wine available. Serving lunch and dinner daily.

The New York Times: Top Pick
The Village Voice: Critics' Pick

Beyoglu

★ **BEST MEDITERRANEAN ON THE UPPER EAST SIDE**

1431 3rd Ave (near 81st St)
New York, NY 10028
(212) 650-0850

Neighborhood Map: **Upper East Side**
Categories: **Mediterranean, Middle Eastern, Small Plates, Turkish**
Price Range: **$$**

These Mediterranean *mezes* (small plates) will leave you begging for more. Try one of the fish specials. Full bar. Serving lunch, dinner and late-night daily.

The New York Times: Top Pick
New York magazine: Critics' Pick
Zagat: 21 food rating (very good to excellent)

Big Nick's Burger and Pizza Joint

★ **BEST BURGERS ON THE UPPER WEST SIDE**

2175 Broadway (near 77th St)
New York, NY 10024
(212) 362-9238

Neighborhood Map: **Upper West Side**
Categories: **American Traditional, Breakfast, Burgers, Italian, Pizza**
Price Range: **$$**
www.bignicksnyc.com

Any place that has everything from veal Parmesan to chicken potpie 24 hours a day is a winner with us. Despite the near 30-page menu of choices, the burgers and pizza are still the best bets at this whimsically dingy New York institution, open since 1962. Beer and wine available. Open 24 hours.

Zagat: 17 food rating (good to very good)

Big Wong

★ **BEST CHINESE IN CHINATOWN**

67 Mott St (bet Bayard and Canal Sts)
New York, NY 10013
(212) 964-0540

Neighborhood Map: **Chinatown**
Category: **Chinese**
Price Range: **$**

This Chinatown institution is famous for its congee and duck dishes. Beer available. Cash only. Serving breakfast, lunch and dinner daily.

The New York Times: Top Pick
Zagat: 22 food rating (very good to excellent)

Billy's Bakery

★ **BEST DESSERT IN CHELSEA**

184 9th Ave (bet 21st and 22nd Sts)
New York, NY 10011
(212) 647-9956

THE BEST RESTAURANTS

Neighborhood Map: **Chelsea**
Categories: **Bakery, Dessert**
Price Range: **$**

With cupcakes rivaling Magnolia Bakery's, Billy's should be
required eating for the sweet-tooth afflicted. No alcohol
available. Serving during breakfast, lunch and dinner hours
daily, late-night Fri–Sat.

Blaue Gans

139 Duane St (bet W Broadway and Church St)
New York, NY 10013
(212) 571-8880

Neighborhood Map: **TriBeCa**
Categories: **Austrian, Brunch, German**
Price Range: **$$$**
www.wallse.com

Casual Austro-German bistro ("Blaue Gans" translates to
"blue goose") with a long zinc dining bar and walls covered
with vintage film and art posters. Full bar. Serving breakfast,
lunch, dinner and late-night daily. Sat–Sun brunch.

The New York Times: ★ (good); Top Pick
New York magazine: Critics' Pick
Zagat: 21 food rating (very good to excellent)

NEW YORK CITY
★TOP100 BLT Steak

106 E 57th St (bet Lexington and Park Aves)
New York, NY 10022
(212) 752-7470

Neighborhood Map: **Midtown East/Murray Hill**
Category: **Steak House**
Price Range: **$$$$**
www.bltsteak.com

BLT Steak was the first among a growing number of "B-L-
T-eateries" in Manhattan, including the likes of BLT Fish,
BLT Prime, BLT Burger and BLT Market. The man behind the
eponymous initials, Laurent Tourondel (the "B" in his BLT
stands for Bistro), who previously was the chef at Cello,

shoots for a modern take on the American steak house with this venture. The dining room, more stylish and welcoming than the dimly lit, wood-paneled meat museums of old, has helped make the restaurant a smashing success since 2004. But not to worry, red meat lovers: Despite the chic digs and the chef's extensive French training, there are plenty of classic cuts to choose from, including the 40-ounce porterhouse for two, the Kobe strip steak (the real deal, from Japan) and the hanger steak, all of which come with your sauce of choice, from Béarnaise to blue cheese or horseradish. Spuds and other sides get the classic à la carte treatment. If you're feeling particularly self-indulgent during lunch hours, BLT unsurprisingly offers a BLT, but this one's made with foie gras and American Kobe steak. Reservations suggested. Full bar. Serving lunch Mon–Fri, dinner Mon–Sat. Closed Sun.

The New York Times: ★★ (very good); Top Pick
New York magazine: ★★ (very good); Critics' Pick
Zagat: 24 food rating (very good to excellent)
Time Out New York: Critics' Pick

63

NEW YORK CITY
★TOP100 Blue Hill

★ BEST CONTEMPORARY IN GREENWICH VILLAGE
75 Washington Pl (bet 6th Ave and Macdougal St)
New York, NY 10011
(212) 539-1776

Neighborhood Map: **Greenwich Village**
Category: **Contemporary**
Price Range: **$$$**
www.bluehillnyc.com

At Blue Hill, just a block away from Washington Square Park, diners walk down the steps from the street, beyond the curtains and into a garden of earthly delights. Garden being the operative word, since a good deal of the restaurant's bounty comes from Blue Hill Farm in Massachusetts in addition to other Hudson Valley farms. From the complimentary bok choy and heirloom tomato amuse-bouche to the also-complimentary bowl of perfectly ripened plums at the end of the meal, superbly fresh fruits and vegetables are allowed to speak for themselves, and they speak volumes. The dining room has a cozy, low-lit, elegant feel. Though it only seats about 55 and you may have to rub elbows with the diners next to you, the noise level is low and the space welcoming. Dan Barber, the James Beard Foundation's Best Chef: New York in 2006, designs seasonally changing menus that may include grilled cobia with curried almonds and vegetables, pastured veal or the standout succulent, creamy farro with baby lamb shank. For dessert, fruit and gourmet ice creams take center stage in dishes such as blackberry cheesecake and corn-flavored ice cream, or blueberry shortcake with brown sugar ice cream. No matter the dish, the commitment to local sourcing shines through with simple preparations yet robust flavors. Reservations suggested. Full bar. Serving dinner nightly.

Michelin Guide: ★ (a very good restaurant in its category)
The New York Times: ★★★ (excellent)
New York magazine: ★★★ (generally excellent); Critics' Pick
Zagat: 26 food rating (extraordinary to perfection)
Time Out New York: Critics' Pick

Blue Ribbon Brasserie

★ **BEST AMERICAN TRADITIONAL IN BROOKLYN**

Neighborhood Map: **Brooklyn (Park Slope)**
280 5th Ave (bet 1st St and Garfield Pl)
Brooklyn, NY 11215
(718) 840-0404

★ **BEST AMERICAN TRADITIONAL IN SOHO**

Neighborhood Map: **SoHo**
97 Sullivan St (bet Spring and Prince Sts)
New York, NY 10012
(212) 274-0404

Categories: **American Traditional, Contemporary, Seafood**
Price Range: **$$$**
www.blueribbonrestaurants.com

The much-loved Manhattan original and its Brooklyn outpost — you won't find a better meal in Park Slope or SoHo. Try the beef marrow and oxtail marmalade appetizer. Full bar. Serving dinner and late-night nightly.

Zagat: 24 food rating (very good to excellent)
Time Out New York: Critics' Pick

NEW YORK CITY

★TOP100 Blue Ribbon Sushi/Blue Ribbon Sushi Bar & Grill

★ **BEST JAPANESE/SUSHI IN BROOKLYN**

Neighborhood Map: **Brooklyn (Park Slope)**
278 5th Ave (bet 1st St and Garfield Pl)
Brooklyn, NY 11215
(718) 840-0408

Neighborhood Map: **Midtown West/Theater District**
308 W 58th St (6 Columbus hotel, Columbus Cir)
New York, NY 10019
(212) 397-0404

★ **BEST JAPANESE/SUSHI IN SOHO**

Neighborhood Map: **SoHo**
119 Sullivan St (bet Spring and Prince Sts)
New York, NY 10012
(212) 343-0404

Category: **Japanese/Sushi**
Price Range: **$$$**
www.blueribbonrestaurants.com

65

Another stronghold in the Bromberg brothers' exceptional local restaurant federation, Blue Ribbon Sushi successfully conquers the raw fish niche with chef Toshi Ueki behind the bar. That's the sushi bar, of course, the best place to grab a seat in either the SoHo or Park Slope locations — both equally hip and, consequently, equally packed — for a taste of *omakase* (chef's choice). But whether it's the conventional spicy tuna, the specialty Blue Ribbon roll (featuring lobster and black caviar) or another choice from the extensive menu of soups, appetizers, maki, sashimi and a rotating variety of daily specials, rest assured that some of the freshest catches from the Atlantic, Pacific and Sea of Japan will be beautifully presented for your palatal enjoyment. The excellent sake selection sweetens the pot. The Midtown location offers traditional brasserie favorites in addition to the sushi. Beer, wine and sake available. SoHo location serving lunch, dinner and late-night daily. Brooklyn location serving dinner and late-night nightly. Midtown location serving breakfast, lunch, dinner and late-night daily.

The New York Times: ★★ (very good); Top Pick
Zagat: 26 food rating (extraordinary to perfection)
Time Out New York: Critics' Pick

Blue Smoke

★ BEST BARBECUE IN GRAMERCY/MADISON PARK

116 E 27th St (near Park Ave)
New York, NY 10016
(212) 447-7733

Neighborhood Map: **Gramercy/Madison Park**
Categories: **Barbecue, Burgers**
Price Range: **$$**
www.bluesmoke.com

Pit-smoked barbecue specialties, from St. Louis and Memphis styles to Texas and Kansas City favorites, are the name of the game at Blue Smoke. The burgers and the mac and cheese are crowd favorites as well. After your meal, head downstairs to the Jazz Standard for live music. Full bar. Serving lunch and dinner daily, late-night Sat–Sun.

The New York Times: ★ (good); Top Pick
New York magazine: Critics' Pick
Zagat: 21 food rating (very good to excellent)
Time Out New York: Critics' Pick

66

Bonita

Neighborhood Map: **Brooklyn (Fort Greene)**
243 Dekalb Ave (near Vanderbilt Ave)
Brooklyn, NY 11205
(718) 622-5300

Neighborhood Map: **Brooklyn (Willamsburg)**
338 Bedford Ave (near S 3rd St)
Brooklyn, NY 11211
(718) 384-9500

Categories: **Brunch, Burritos, Mexican**
Price Range: **$$**
www.bonitanyc.com

Tasty burritos and a popular weekend brunch make these two Brooklyn Mexican spots major winners. Full bar at Dekalb location. Beer and wine available at Bedford location. Serving lunch Mon–Fri, dinner nightly. Sat–Sun brunch. Hours vary by location.

Zagat: 19 food rating (good to very good)
Time Out New York: Critics' Pick

NEW YORK CITY
★TOP100 **Boqueria**

★ **BEST SPANISH IN UNION SQUARE/FLATIRON**
53 W 19th St (near 6th Ave)
New York, NY 10011
(212) 255-4160

Neighborhood Map: **Union Square/Flatiron**
Categories: **Brunch, Small Plates, Spanish**
Price Range: **$$**
www.boquerianyc.com

This stylish gem on 19th Street reclaims tapas for the Spanish
cause. Just a few blocks from the ultra-crowded heavy hitters
around Union Square (Gramercy Tavern, Union Square Cafe,
Craft), Boqueria occupies a much-needed neighborhood
restaurant niche, with its casual, unrushed atmosphere. Tall,
wooden tables populate the middle of the dining room, while
long, elevated booths line each wall of the narrow, beige-
colored space. Late-twenty-somethings, European couples
and the bar crowd coexist seamlessly. Cured meats, specialty
cheeses and Spanish small plates are the order of the day
from chef/partner Seamus Mullen (Irish by birth, Spanish
by training and heart). The supremely rich bacon-wrapped
date stuffed with almonds and Valdéon cheese might knock
you out of your chair, while *salchichón* (spiced pork sausage
cured with garlic and herbs) and *jamon* serrano (15-month
aged Spanish ham) are among pork treatments. Larger plates
include paella and roasted skirt steak. Reservations not
accepted. Full bar. Serving lunch, dinner and late-night daily.
Sat–Sun brunch noon–5 pm.

The New York Times: ★★ (very good); Top Pick
New York magazine: ★★ (very good); Critics' Pick
Zagat: 22 food rating (very good to excellent)
The Village Voice: Critics' Pick

67

NEW YORK CITY
★TOP100 **Bouley**

163 Duane St (near Hudson St)
New York, NY 10013
(212) 964-2525

Neighborhood Map: **TriBeCa**
Categories: **Contemporary, French**

Price Range: **$$$$**
www.davidbouley.com

The rather trying evolution of august chef David Bouley's
namesake TriBeCa restaurant aptly illustrates why most
simply can't cut it in the major leagues — and that the ones
who survive make Manhattan the top dining destination in the
country. From a 9/11 closure to a significant staff turnover,
Bouley's envisioned culinary empire seemed doomed when
The New York Times stripped away that coveted fourth star
in 2004. But the controversial, reserved Connecticut native
took a deep breath, fell back on his French grandmother's
teachings, and kept cooking his progressive French dishes
with his signature moxie for tropical flavors. Chef Bouley has
since emerged from the ashes, reborn and perhaps better
than ever, proudly baring the unparalleled clarity of flavor and
concept that won his original loyal following and that has since
secured him a great deal more. The restaurant's new digs
(French château-style complete with ornate, hand-painted
walls), just around the corner from the old space, give diners
an even more lavish Bouley experience. Full bar. Serving lunch
and dinner daily. Reservations not accepted. Full bar. Serving
dinner Mon–Sat. Sat–Sun brunch.

The New York Times: ★★★ (excellent); Top Pick
New York magazine: ★★ (very good); Critics' Pick
Zagat: 28 food rating (extraordinary to perfection)
Time Out New York: Critics' Pick

Bouley Upstairs

130 W Broadway (near Duane St)
New York, NY 10013
(212) 608-5829

Neighborhood Map: **TriBeCa**
Categories: **Brunch, Contemporary, Japanese/Sushi**
Price Range: **$$$**
www.davidbouley.com

"A quirky hodgepodge of a place," as *New York* magazine
has put it, that features a sushi bar, salads, Japanese hors
d'oeuvres and the Bouley Burger. A recent expansion adds to
its appeal. Reservations not accepted. Full bar. Serving dinner
Mon–Sat. Sat brunch 11 am–3 pm, Sun brunch 11 am–4 pm.

The New York Times: ★★ (very good); Top Pick

New York magazine: ★★ (very good); Critics' Pick
Zagat: 25 food rating (very good to excellent)

Bread & Olive

★ BEST MIDDLE EASTERN IN THE FINANCIAL DISTRICT
Neighborhood Map: **Financial District**
20 John St (near Broadway)
New York, NY 10038
(212) 385-2144

Neighborhood Map: **Midtown West/Theater District**
24 W 45th St (near 5th Ave)
New York, NY 10036
(212) 764-1588

Category: **Middle Eastern**
Price Range: **$$**
www.breadnolive.com

Self-billed as "The Middle Eastern Place," this Midtown
Manhattan favorite features a mighty offering of vegetarian
appetizer platters, including baba ganoush, and some of
the best chicken *shawarma* you'll ever taste. No alcohol
available. BYOB. Serving lunch and early dinner Mon–Fri.
Closed Sat–Sun.

New York magazine: Critics' Pick
The Village Voice: Critics' Pick

Bread Tribeca

301 Church St (near Walker St)
New York, NY 10013
(212) 334-8282

Neighborhood Map: **TriBeCa**
Categories: **Brunch, Italian**
Price Range: **$$$**
www.breadtribeca.com

Bread Tribeca serves hearty Italian food of unsparing
proportions in a modern dining room, where Italian-themed
movies play on the bar TV. Full bar. Serving lunch and dinner
daily, late-night Fri–Sat. Sat–Sun brunch.

69

WHERE THE LOCALS EAT™

The New York Times: ★★ (very good); Top Pick
New York magazine: ★ (good); Critics' Pick
Zagat: 19 food rating (good to very good)
Time Out New York: Critics' Pick

Bridge Cafe

★ **BEST AMERICAN TRADITIONAL IN THE FINANCIAL DISTRICT**

279 Water St (near Dover St)
New York, NY 10038
(212) 227-3344

Neighborhood Map: **Financial District**
Categories: **American Traditional, Brunch**
Price Range: **$$$**
www.eatgoodinny.com/New.York

With its claim as "the oldest drinking establishment in New York" — the building has housed some sort of drinking/eating establishment throughout its history, since 1794 — Bridge Cafe also boasts excellent renditions of American favorites, including a stellar buffalo steak. Reservations suggested. Full bar. Serving lunch and dinner daily, late-night Fri–Sat. Sun brunch 11:45 am–4 pm.

New York magazine: Critics' Pick
Zagat: 21 food rating (very good to excellent)

Brown Café

★ **BEST CAFÉ ON THE LOWER EAST SIDE**

61 Hester St (bet Essex and Ludlow Sts)
New York, NY 10002
(212) 477-2427

Neighborhood Map: **Lower East Side**
Categories: **Breakfast, Café**
Price Range: **$$**
www.greenbrownorange.com

Attention to detail makes this cozy neighborhood spot special, as farm-to-table ingredients ensure quality breakfasts, popular specialty sandwiches and eye-opening coffee. Owner Alejandro Alcocer even built the wooden tables and chairs himself. Beer and wine available. Serving breakfast, lunch and dinner daily. Closes 6 pm Mon and Sun.

70

The New York Times: Top Pick
Zagat: 22 food rating (very good to excellent)
Time Out New York: Critics' Pick

NEW YORK CITY
★TOP100 Burger Joint at Le Parker Meridien

★ BEST BURGERS IN NYC

119 W 56th St (bet 6th and 7th Aves, Le Parker Meridien hotel)
New York, NY 10019
(212) 708-7414

Neighborhood Map: **Midtown West/Theater District**
Categories: **Burgers, Hotel Restaurant**
Price Range: **$**
www.parkermeridien.com/eat4.php

For most burger connoisseurs, there's not much enthusiasm
for formerly frozen fast food burgers, and $30 bistro burgers
dressed with foie gras or the aioli du jour somehow seem to
miss the point. True burger bliss lies somewhere in between.
Thankfully, the Burger Joint at Le Parker Meridien provides
a happy medium, achieving the ideal balance of simplicity
with fresh, quality ingredients and a backyard taste. From
the elegant lobby of the four-star hotel, just look for the
small, neon burger light on the wall. You'll pass through a
dark hallway and some black curtains before running smack
dab into the line. (Despite the lack of signage and its unlikely
location, the line will attest that this is no longer a secret
among Midtown burger enthusiasts.) The limited décor
approximates a '70s dive of sorts, with red vinyl booths, wood
paneling, various knickknacks (see Louie Anderson and Rudy
Giuliani bobblehead dolls above the counter) and burgers
that come wrapped in white paper. Thin, crispy fries come
in a brown bag. The small but thick burgers come cooked
to order, and toppings consist of lettuce, tomato, ketchup,
pickles, mayo and mustard. For everything, just say "the
works" to keep the line moving — signs threaten that you will
be skipped if you're not ready to order. Wash it all down with
a thick milk shake or a pitcher of Sam Adams poured in clear
plastic cups among friends. If there are no seats, a short walk
to Central Park is a fine alternative. Beer available. Serving
lunch and dinner daily, late-night Fri–Sat.

New York magazine: Critics' Pick

71

Zagat: 23 food rating (very good to excellent)
Time Out New York: Critics' Pick

NEW YORK CITY
★TOP100 Café Boulud

20 E 76th St (bet 5th and Madison Aves)
New York, NY 10021
(212) 772-2600

Neighborhood Map: **Upper East Side**
Categories: **Brunch, French**
Price Range: **$$$**
www.danielnyc.com/cafeboulud

The little sister of world-renowned Daniel, Café Boulud
is truly a family restaurant, as the original café in Lyon,
France, was opened and passed down by the chef's great
grandparents. But this stylish uptown café plays no Jan Brady
to Daniel's Marsha. Instead, it diverges from the original,
with a slightly more relaxed atmosphere (still not for the
paupers) and playful, globetrotting cuisine. A few expected
French classics appear (foie gras, seared arctic char) under
the La Tradition portion of the menu, while the rest of the
offerings are divided into Le Voyage (world cuisine), Le
Potager (vegetables inspired by the market), La Collection (a
tasting menu for the whole table) and La Saison (flavors of
the season). The antithesis of stuffy or pretentious, inventive
plates may include anything from Moroccan spiced duck and
Thai lobster (with a coconut lemongrass sauce and Thai basil)
to corn risotto and other worthy pasta offerings. You might
need a special occasion or particularly good day at the race
track to justify Daniel, but there's always an excuse to reap
the rewards of a four-star chef at play at Café Boulud. Jacket
suggested. Reservations suggested. Full bar. Serving lunch
Tue–Sat, dinner nightly. Sun brunch 11:30 am–2:30 pm.

Michelin Guide: ★ (a very good restaurant in its category)
The New York Times: ★★★ (excellent); Top Pick
New York magazine: ★★★ (generally excellent); Critics' Pick
Zagat: 27 food rating (extraordinary to perfection)
The Village Voice: Critics' Pick

Cafe Colonial

★ **BEST LATIN/SOUTH AMERICAN IN LITTLE ITALY/NOLITA**

72

276 Elizabeth St (near Houston St)
New York, NY 10012
(212) 274-0044

Neighborhood Map: **Little Italy/NoLita**
Categories: **Breakfast, Brunch, Latin/South American**
Price Range: **$$**
www.cafecolonialny.com

A tiny, trendy Brazilian restaurant, Cafe Colonial draws long
lines for weekend brunches with banana French toast and
a variety of omelets. Full bar. Serving breakfast, lunch and
dinner daily, late-night Fri–Sat. Sat–Sun brunch 8 am–4 pm.

Zagat: 18 food rating (good to very good)

NEW YORK CITY
★TOP100 Café des Artistes

1 W 67th St (near Central Park W)
New York, NY 10023
(212) 877-3500

Neighborhood Map: **Upper West Side**
Categories: **Brunch, French**
Price Range: **$$$**
www.cafenyc.com

73

Located just four blocks from Lincoln Center and 10 minutes
from the theater district, this café is the kind of place that would
have been perfect for a game of hide-and-seek when you were
a kid, what with its creaky charm and accompanying nooks and
crannies. As an adult, you'll go for the dependably classic food,
the experience of dining in a charming, historic haunt open since
1917, and perhaps the chance to spy celebrity regulars among
other thoroughbred Manhattanites who consider this a favorite
neighborhood haven. (It was a favorite of the late Paul Newman.)
At one time, artists of every stripe lived, worked and ate in the
buildings on the block where the café sits, and the restaurant was
a popular gathering place known for hearty, reasonably priced
food, good drink and, not least, social stimulation. In that regard,
not much has changed. Sitting among the pastel murals of artist
Howard Chandler Christy, settle in with one of the old-fashioned
named cocktails such as Fall, a mixture of Imperia vodka and
apple liquor garnished with a fresh apple slice, and consider the
bistro menu that's all humble splendor and no fad. Enjoy the
oven-roasted organic chicken with mashed potatoes, asparagus

and beurre blanc sauce or order the favorite steak frites. Jacket preferred but not required. Full bar. Serving dinner nightly. Sat brunch 11 am–3 pm and Sun brunch 10 am–3 pm.

Zagat: 22 food rating (very good to excellent)

Cafe el Portal

174 Elizabeth St (near Spring St)
New York, NY 10012
(212) 226-4642

Neighborhood Map: **Little Italy/NoLita**
Categories: **Burritos, Mexican**
Price Range: **$$**

This tiny, teal-colored dining room turns out authentic Mexican fare at very reasonable prices. Patrons pack this no-longer-hidden gem for fresh guacamole and chips, fish tacos, and standout chile rellenos. Full bar. Serving lunch, dinner and late-night Mon–Sat. Closed Sun.

Time Out New York: Critics' Pick

74

NEW YORK CITY **★TOP100** Cafe Fiorello

1900 Broadway (bet 63rd and 64th Sts)
New York, NY 10023
(212) 595-5330

Neighborhood Map: **Upper West Side**
Categories: **Brunch, Italian, Pizza**
Price Range: **$$$**
www.cafefiorello.com

The perfect spot for a pre- or post-show meal — provided that Wagner's *Siegfried* hasn't cost you your appetite — Cafe Fiorello, which has been open more than 30 years, stakes its claim as "The Longest Running Show on Broadway." The spacious, mirror- and dark wood-laden interior and ever-popular sidewalk dining attract a mix of devoted regulars, tourists, opera/ballet/theater fans and even a few folks in the biz, given its proximity to Lincoln Center. The centerpiece of the restaurant, the antipasti bar, features more than 30 selections, but for some, it's the thin-crust pizzas that steal the show (the prosciutto di Parma or wild mushroom and buffalo mozzarella pies, for example). Classics such as the signature open-faced lasagna and veal scaloppini keep the traditionalists satisfied. Full bar. Serving lunch Mon–Fri, dinner nightly. Late-night Mon–Sat. Sat–Sun brunch 10 am–3 pm.

Zagat: 20 food rating (very good to excellent)

NEW YORK CITY
⭐TOP100 Café Habana/Habana Outpost

★ **BEST CUBAN IN NYC**
Neighborhood Map: **Little Italy/NoLita**
17 Prince St (near Elizabeth St)
New York, NY 10012
(212) 625-2001

Neighborhood Map: **Brooklyn (Fort Greene)**
757 Fulton St (near S Portland Ave)
Brooklyn, NY 11217
(718) 858-9500

75

Categories: **Breakfast, Brunch, Cuban**
Price Range: **$$**
www.habanaoutpost.com

Devoted masses line the sidewalk outside this south-of-the-border standout north of Little Italy. This tiny chrome luncheonette's popularity is no surprise, given its festive atmosphere and extensive menu of affordable Cuban and central Mexican fare. Dive right into one of the city's best mojitos or a frozen guava margarita, and be sure to order the locally famed grilled corn prepared Mexican-style (with chili powder, lime and cheese). The menu offers everything from steak and eggs and huevos rancheros at breakfast to lunch and dinner favorites such as Baja fish tacos with battered catfish, skirt steak with rice and beans, and steamed mussels in a white wine, leek and coconut sauce. Next door, the to-go counter is a go-to option for those wanting to avoid the lines or the general temptation of a good time. The aggressively green sister location, Habana Outpost in Brooklyn, claims to be the first solar-powered restaurant in New York. This eco-eatery is something of a sustainable-living-themed amusement park, with movie nights, educational programs, and (on weekends) a market for local vendors and artists.

Full bar. Café serving breakfast, lunch, dinner and late-night daily. Habana Outpost serving lunch, dinner and late-night Wed–Mon. Closed Tue.

New York magazine: Critics' Pick
Zagat: 20 food rating (very good to excellent)
Time Out New York: Critics' Pick

NEW YORK CITY
★TOP100 Cafe Luxembourg

★ **BEST BISTRO IN NYC**

200 W 70th St (bet Amsterdam and West End Aves)
New York, NY 10023
(212) 873-7411

Neighborhood Map: **Upper West Side**
Categories: **Bistro, Breakfast, Brunch, French**
Price Range: **$$$**
www.cafeluxembourg.com

An Upper West Side staple since 1983, Cafe Luxembourg epitomizes the ideal neighborhood bistro. Whether a classic rendition of steak frites at lunch, duck hash with eggs in the morning, or the frozen banana pecan soufflé after a night at the theater, menu options accommodate nearly any dining circumstance. Antique mirrors, white-papered tabletops and red leather banquettes adorn the dining room, which is filled with a mix of theatergoers, longtime regulars, Francophiles and even a celebrity or two from time to time. Other bistro favorites include crispy skate and Long Island duck breast with escarole. Have a glass of Bordeaux and a plate of cheese, twirl your mustache, and direct your best "haw haw haw" toward the foolish Yanks who are missing out and fighting the crowds downtown instead. Reservations suggested. Full bar. Serving breakfast, lunch and dinner daily. Late-night Mon–Sat. Sat–Sun brunch.

The New York Times: ★ (good)
New York magazine: Critics' Pick
Zagat: 20 food rating (very good to excellent)
Time Out New York: Critics' Pick

NEW YORK CITY
★TOP100 Cafe Mogador

★ **BEST MOROCCAN IN NYC**

76

101 St. Marks Pl (bet 1st Ave and Ave A)
New York, NY 10009
(212) 677-2226

Neighborhood Map: **East Village/NoHo**
Categories: **Breakfast, Brunch, Mediterranean, Middle
   Eastern, Moroccan**
Price Range: **$$**
www.cafemogador.com

Cafe Mogador is a mecca for students, a diverse international
crowd and other generally hip East Village types. A perfect
neighborhood spot for relaxing and sipping on some
Moroccan tea, Turkish coffee or a glass of wine (while you
study, of course), Mogador sports a handful of sidewalk tables
looking out onto St. Mark's Place. A few steps down from the
street, the main dining room exudes a relaxed café feel, with
cream-colored walls and green trim, hanging lamps, wine
racks, and chalkboards showing the daily specials. The menu
consists of Moroccan and some Middle Eastern classics such
as falafel, a few varieties of couscous, and hummus with a
spicy crushed red pepper and olive oil mixture on the side.
Tagines, slow-simmered spiced stews, are the best-selling
item and come with lamb (on the bone) or chicken, and
rice or couscous, in a choice of five different sauces — try
the spicy, green *charmoula* on a cold, rainy day for soul-
affirming inner warmness. Breakfast draws a crowd as well
with creative offerings, including Moroccan eggs (poached
with a spicy tomato sauce, home fries and pita) or the Foul
Madamez, a hard-boiled egg with fava beans and hummus. Full
bar. Serving breakfast Mon–Fri, lunch, dinner and late-night
daily. Sat–Sun brunch 9 am–4 pm.

The New York Times: Top Pick
Zagat: 21 food rating (very good to excellent)
Time Out New York: Critics' Pick

77

NEW YORK CITY
★TOP100 Calle Ocho

★ **BEST LATIN/SOUTH AMERICAN ON THE UPPER WEST SIDE**
446 Columbus Ave (bet 81st and 82nd Sts)
New York, NY 10024
(212) 873-5025

Neighborhood Map: **Upper West Side**
Categories: **Brunch, Latin/South American**

Price Range: **$$$**
www.calleochonyc.com

If Ricky Martin gave the Nuevo Latino invasion a bad name, then Calle Ocho restored its dignity (and proved to have far greater staying power, having eclipsed the 10-year mark recently). This slick, vibrant spot delivers some much-needed livelihood to the Upper West Side. Salsa music blares over the loud conversation of the young, pretty crowd swarming the bar area, and high ceilings, brick archways and bright rooster murals on the walls enhance the festive atmosphere. Specialty cocktails abound at the bar: *caipirinhas, cojitos* (coconut rum, lime juice, mint and sugar) and tropical daiquiris are among the selections. Starters shine here as well, from multiple varieties of ceviche and *tiraditos* to fire-roasted sweet corn empanadas and bacon-wrapped stuffed dates. Similarly colorful entrées such as paella, *ropa vieja* and *mojo*-braised pork shank celebrate multiple culinary traditions of the Latin world, from Colombia and Cuba to Costa Rica and Spain. A number of coffee drinks and deluxe desserts — flan with whipped sour cream, toasted coconut ice cream with a chocolate shell and pineapple sauce — provide a memorable finish. Full bar. Serving dinner nightly. Late-night Sat–Sun. Sun brunch 11:30 am–3 pm.

The New York Times: ★ (good)
New York magazine: Critics' Pick
Zagat: 22 food rating (very good to excellent)
Time Out New York: Critics' Pick

Candle Cafe/Candle 79

★ **BEST VEGETARIAN ON THE UPPER EAST SIDE**
Neighborhood Map: **Upper East Side**
1307 3rd Ave (bet 74th and 75th Sts)
New York, NY 10021
(212) 472-0970

Neighborhood Map: **Upper East Side**
154 E 79th St (near Lexington Ave)
New York, NY 10075
(212) 537-7179

Categories: **Brunch, Vegetarian**
Price Range: **$$**
www.candlecafe.com

If four-legged creatures could toast this place, they would. Both Candle outposts are many a non-meat-eaters' picks for best vegetarian and vegan food in New York City. Reservations suggested. Beer, wine and sake available. Serving lunch and dinner daily. Sat–Sun brunch, at Candle 79 only, noon–4pm.

The New York Times: Top Pick
Zagat: 23 food rating (very good to excellent)

Caracas Arepa Bar

★ **BEST LATIN/SOUTH AMERICAN IN THE EAST VILLAGE/ NOHO**
93 1/2 E 7th St (bet 1st Ave and Ave A)
New York, NY 10009
(212) 529-2314

Neighborhood Map: **East Village/NoHo**
Categories: **Brunch, Latin/South American**
Price Range: **$**
www.caracasarepabar.com

79

This tiny Venezuelan restaurant packs in diners for the signature arepas — corn flour sandwiches of sorts filled with a variety of meats, cheese and vegetables. Beer available. Serving dinner nightly. Sat–Sun brunch starting at noon.

The New York Times: Top Pick
New York magazine: Critics' Pick
Zagat: 25 food rating (very good to excellent)
Time Out New York: Critics' Pick

NEW YORK CITY ★**TOP100** Carl's Steaks

★ **BEST CHEESE STEAKS IN NYC**
Neighborhood Map: **Midtown East/Murray Hill**
507 3rd Ave (near 34th St)
New York, NY 10016
(212) 696-5336

Neighborhood Map: **TriBeCa**
79 Chambers St (near Broadway)
New York, NY 10007
(212) 566-2828

Category: **Cheese Steaks**
Price Range: **$**
www.carlsteaks.com

Carl's Steaks brings some brotherly love to the Big Apple,
sharing Philadelphia's most renowned culinary (and perhaps
cultural) contribution with New Yorkers. This Murray Hill
neighborhood staple (there's also one in TriBeCa) is perfect
for late-night noshing (open until 4:30 am on weekends) or
for fulfilling any craving for greasy goodness. Though a veggie
sandwich, a low-carb cheese steak platter (no bun) and chili
cheese fries are available, the draw here is the substantial
hoagie roll topped with sliced sirloin, grilled onions and
cheese. American and provolone cheeses are available, but
the processed Cheez Whiz is the legit way to go. Mushrooms,
peppers, tomatoes and lettuce are add-ons. No alcohol
available. Serving lunch, dinner and late-night daily.

New York magazine: Critics' Pick
Zagat: 21 food rating (very good to excellent)

Casa Mono

★ **BEST SMALL PLATES IN UNION SQUARE/FLATIRON**
52 Irving Pl (near 17th St)
New York, NY 10003
(212) 253-2773

Neighborhood Map: **Union Square/Flatiron**
Categories: **Small Plates, Spanish**
Price Range: **$$$**
www.casamononyc.com

Casa Mono features *raciones* of Catalan specialties and
serves dishes from all corners of Spain. Reservations
suggested. Beer and wine available. Serving lunch, dinner
and late-night daily.

The New York Times: Top Pick
New York magazine: ★★ (very good); Critics' Pick
Zagat: 25 food rating (very good to excellent)
Time Out New York: Critics' Pick

Celeste

502 Amsterdam Ave (near 84th St)

New York, NY 10024
(212) 874-4559

Neighborhood Map: **Upper West Side**
Categories: **Brunch, Italian**
Price Range: **$$**

No longer a secret, this not-so-hidden gem packs patrons in
for pastas made fresh daily, pizzas from the wood-burning
oven and creative antipasti offerings. Don't pass up the gelato.
Beer and wine available. Cash only. Serving dinner nightly.
Sat–Sun brunch.

The New York Times: Top Pick
New York magazine: Critics' Pick
Zagat: 24 food rating (very good to excellent)

NEW YORK CITY **★TOP100** 'Cesca

★ **BEST ITALIAN ON THE UPPER WEST SIDE**
164 W 75th St (near Amsterdam Ave)
New York, NY 10024
(212) 787-6300

Neighborhood Map: **Upper West Side**
Categories: **Brunch, Italian**
Price Range: **$$$**
www.cescanyc.com

Before the southern Italian food can sweep you off your feet,
the dining room at this Upper West Side favorite (opened in
2003 and named for a partner's daughter, Francesca) seduces
visitors with its warm woods, open floor plan, luscious brown
fabrics and soft light from custom-made iron lamps. Chef
Kevin Garcia's straightforward menu includes daily specials
(or *piatti del giorno*) and a three-course pre-theater offering,
with choice of salad, entrée and dessert (buffalo mozzarella,
pollo al mosto and gelati, for example). 'Cesca makes its
expertly seasoned pork sausage in-house and offers rustic
side items with which no *paesano* could find fault: brussels
sprouts, roast potatoes and Tuscan herb fries, among others.
If you've no time or money for a trip to Napoli, consider a visit
to 'Cesca to sate the craving for a southern Italian experience.
Full bar. Serving dinner nightly. Sun brunch noon–3 pm.

The New York Times: ★★ (very good)

New York magazine: ★★ (very good); Critics' Pick
Zagat: 23 food rating (very good to excellent)
Time Out New York: Critics' Pick

NEW YORK CITY
★TOP100 Chanterelle

2 Harrison St (near Hudson St)
New York, NY 10013
(212) 966-6960

Neighborhood Map: **TriBeCa**
Category: **French**
Price Range: **$$$$$**
www.chanterellenyc.com

With bohemian beginnings in SoHo, Chanterelle flourished to become one of New York's most renowned fine-dining destinations. Karen and David Waltuck relocated their restaurant to TriBeCa in 1989, but it still possesses that unpretentious, subtle elegance (for this caliber of dining). Among the many accolades piled on Chanterelle is the James Beard Foundation's 2007 Best Chef: New York designation. David's locally sourced, modern French fare changes with the season, so menus are handwritten, and their covers are decorated with the works of artists, photographers and writers such as Roy Lichtenstein, John Cage and Allen Ginsberg. (Past menus are framed and displayed in the reception area.) Waltuck's tasting and prix fixe menus — à la carte is only available at lunch — have included rich, decadent items such as potato "risotto" with sautéed duck foie gras and Berkshire pork loin with muscat, ginger and violet mustard. No detail goes unattended here. And any restaurant that employs a *fromager*, someone to oversee cheese, is a winner in our book. Jacket suggested. Reservations suggested. Full bar with extensive wine list. Serving lunch Thu–Sat, dinner nightly.

The New York Times: ★★★ (excellent); Top Pick
New York magazine: ★★★ (generally excellent); Critics' Pick
Zagat: 27 food rating (extraordinary to perfection)
Time Out New York: Critics' Pick

Charles' Southern-Style Kitchen

★ **BEST SOUTHERN CUISINE IN HARLEM**
2841 Frederick Douglass Blvd (near 151st St)

New York, NY 10039
(212) 926-4313

Neighborhood Map: **Harlem**
Categories: **Buffet/Cafeteria, Fried Chicken, Soul Food, Southern**
Price Range: **$**

North Carolina native Charles Gabriel serves up a bountiful buffet of Southern soul food favorites at Charles' Southern-Style Kitchen. One side of the restaurant is carry-out only, a popular option for those preferring to avoid further temptation. No alcohol available. Serving lunch and dinner Wed–Sun. Closed Mon–Tue.

The New York Times: Top Pick
Zagat: 22 food rating (very good to excellent)

Chat 'n Chew

★ **BEST HOME-STYLE IN UNION SQUARE/FLATIRON**
10 E 16th St (bet Union Sq W and 5th Ave)
New York, NY 10003
(212) 243-1616

Neighborhood Map: **Union Square/Flatiron**
Categories: **American Traditional, Brunch, Home-style**
Price Range: **$$**
www.chatnchew.ypguides.net

Upholding the American values of butter, Häagen-Dazs and the deep fryer, Chat 'n Chew defies trend in favor of tried-and-true Americana, proclaiming, "Peace, love, and macaroni and cheese." Full bar. Serving lunch, dinner and late-night daily. Sat–Sun brunch 11 am–4 pm.

Zagat: 16 food rating (good to very good)
Time Out New York: Critics' Pick

Chino's

173 3rd Ave (near 16th St)
New York, NY 10003
(212) 598-1200

Neighborhood Map: **Gramercy/Madison Park**

83

Categories: **Asian Fusion, Small Plates**
Price Range: **$$**
www.chinosnyc.com

Nothing exemplifies the American model of the melting pot quite like the words "Chinese tapas." Colorful sake cocktails, exotic teas and late-night hours on the weekends add to the appeal. Full bar. Serving dinner nightly, late-night Fri–Sat.

New York magazine: Critics' Pick
Zagat: 19 food rating (good to very good)

ChipShop

★ BEST IRISH/BRITISH IN BROOKLYN
Neighborhood Map: **Brooklyn (Bay Ridge)**
7215 3rd Ave (near 73rd St)
Brooklyn, NY 11209
(718) 748-0594

Neighborhood Map: **Brooklyn (Brooklyn Heights)**
129 Atlantic Ave (near Henry St)
Brooklyn, NY 11201
(718) 855-7775

Neighborhood Map: **Brooklyn (Park Slope)**
383 5th Ave (near 6th St)
Brooklyn, NY 11215
(718) 832-7701

Categories: **Brunch, Fish and Chips, Irish/British**
Price Range: **$$**
www.chipshopnyc.com

Fish and chips and a fried Mars bar? It doesn't get much better than this easy-on-the-wallet Brooklyn favorite (especially for brunch). Cash only at the Park Slope and Bay Ridge locations. Full bar at Brooklyn Heights location. Beer and wine available at Park Slope and Bay Ridge locations. Serving lunch and dinner daily. Sat–Sun brunch at Park Slope and Bay Ridge locations. Hours vary by location.

The New York Times: Top Pick
Zagat: 19 food rating (good to very good)

Clinton St. Baking Company & Restaurant

★ **BEST BREAKFAST ON THE LOWER EAST SIDE**

4 Clinton St (near Houston St)
New York, NY 10002
(646) 602-6263

Neighborhood Map: **Lower East Side**
Categories: **American Traditional, Breakfast, Brunch**
Price Range: **$$**
www.clintonstreetbaking.com

Way more than your average bakery, Clinton St. boasts a fantastic breakfast, including some of the best pancakes around. Full bar. Serving breakfast and lunch daily, dinner Mon–Sat. Sat–Sun brunch.

Zagat: 25 food rating (very good to excellent)
Time Out New York: Critics' Pick

Convivium Osteria

★ **BEST MEDITERRANEAN IN BROOKLYN**

68 5th Ave (bet Bergen St and St. Marks Ave)
Brooklyn, NY 11217
(718) 857-1833

Neighborhood Map: **Brooklyn (Park Slope)**
Categories: **Italian, Mediterranean, Spanish**
Price Range: **$$**
www.convivium-osteria.com

In a rustic but elegant setting, Mediterranean fare shines with authenticity and flavor. Beer and wine available. Serving dinner nightly.

The New York Times: ★ (good); Top Pick
New York magazine: Critics' Pick
Zagat: 25 food rating (very good to excellent)
Time Out New York: Critics' Pick

Cookshop

★ **BEST AMERICAN TRADITIONAL IN CHELSEA**

85

156 10th Ave (near 20th St)
New York, NY 10011
(212) 924-4440

Neighborhood Map: **Chelsea**
Categories: **American Traditional, Breakfast, Brunch, Oysters**
Price Range: **$$$**
www.cookshopny.com

Enjoy traditional American fare with a modern twist at this casual Chelsea restaurant with an open kitchen and outdoor seating. It's particularly popular for brunch, with a stellar rendition of huevos rancheros and a variety of colorful, heavily garnished cocktails. Reservations suggested. Full bar. Serving lunch and breakfast Mon–Fri, dinner nightly. Sat–Sun brunch 11 am–3 pm.

The New York Times: ★★ (very good); Top Pick
New York magazine: Critics' Pick
Zagat: 23 food rating (very good to excellent)

NEW YORK CITY
★TOP100 Corner Bistro

★ BEST BURGERS IN THE WEST VILLAGE/MEATPACKING DISTRICT

331 W 4th St (near Jane St)
New York, NY 10014
(212) 242-9502

Neighborhood Map: **West Village/Meatpacking District**
Category: **Burgers**
Price Range: **$**
http://cornerbistro.ypguides.net

This West Village dive has consistently topped New York City's burger ranks since the '60s. Little appears to have changed in its nearly 50 years. The décor remains dated and a bit dingy, the vibe friendly, and the burgers simple and about as classic as they come: 8-ounce-thick patties topped with American cheese, onions, bacon, lettuce and tomato. In any other town, this type of hole in the wall might be considered a hidden gem, but Corner Bistro has been discovered many times over, as the long lines will attest. It might be wise to come at off-peak hours, or you can strap on your drinking boots and enjoy a draft beer at throwback prices while you wait for your burger. Fries are a worthy accompaniment, as is the chili burger if you're feeling particularly cheeky. Warning: not ideal for vegetarians, carb counters and claustrophobes. Full bar. Cash only. Serving lunch, dinner and late-night daily.

Zagat: 22 food rating (very good to excellent)
Time Out New York: Critics' Pick

NEW YORK CITY
★TOP100 **Craft**

43 E 19th St (bet Park Ave S and Broadway)
New York, NY 10003
(212) 780-0880

Neighborhood Map: **Union Square/Flatiron**
Categories: **Contemporary, Oysters, Seafood**
Price Range: **$$$**
www.craftrestaurant.com

Head judge of Bravo's *Top Chef* series and James Beard award-winning chef status aside, Tom Colicchio is known locally as a culinary god. The refined simplicity of his contemporary menus and his almost obsessive commitment to the world's purest ingredients come to the second of his ventures (the first being Union Square's fair-haired Gramercy Tavern). Craft's debut left many diners stunned by the true à la carte dining approach. But Colicchio's kitchen makes build-your-own plate a build-your-own adventure, each bite of preferred protein and sides revealing an exciting burst of sublime flavor. From black bass to beef tongue, braised is best, but it's hard to go wrong with such expert execution. Reservations required. Full bar. Serving lunch Mon–Fri, dinner nightly.

The New York Times: ★★★ (excellent); Top Pick
New York magazine: ★★★★ (exceptional; consistently elite); Critics' Pick
Zagat: 26 food rating (extraordinary to perfection)
Time Out New York: Critics' Pick

Cru

24 5th Ave (near 9th St)
New York, NY 10011
(212) 529-1700

Neighborhood Map: **Greenwich Village**
Category: **Contemporary**
Price Range: **$$$$$**
www.cru-nyc.com

Very fine wines and somehow even finer food are served here
in the heart of Greenwich Village. Reservations suggested.
Full bar. Serving dinner Mon–Sat. Closed Sun.

Michelin Guide: ★ (a very good restaurant in its category)
The New York Times: ★★★ (excellent); Top Pick
New York magazine: ★★★ (generally excellent); Critics' Pick
Zagat: 26 food rating (extraordinary to perfection)
Time Out New York: Critics' Pick

Da Umberto
107 W 17th St (bet 6th and 7th Aves)
New York, NY 10011
(212) 989-0303

Neighborhood Map: **Chelsea**
Category: **Italian**
Price Range: **$$$**

Classy yet unpretentious, Da Umberto has earned a devoted
following with its Old World charm and authentic Tuscan
cuisine. Reservations required. Full bar. Serving lunch Mon–
Fri, dinner Mon–Sat. Closed Sun.

Zagat: 25 food rating (very good to excellent)

NEW YORK CITY ★**TOP100** Daniel
★ **BEST FRENCH IN NYC**
60 E 65th St (near Madison Ave)
New York, NY 10065
(212) 288-0033

Neighborhood Map: **Upper East Side**
Category: **French**
Price Range: **$$$$$**
www.danielnyc.com

This *New York Times* four-star, Michelin two-star, Relais

& Chateaux establishment has topped nearly every major publication's list of the best restaurants in America, including *Food & Wine*, *Bon Appétit* and *Esquire* magazines as well as the *International Herald Tribune* and culturally attuned *Playboy*. But the crème de la crème of haute French dining offers the kind of seduction that cannot be denoted by any sort of award, no matter how prestigious. Chef Daniel Boulud aims to alight all the senses, bringing sensual genius and gastronomic sex appeal to his Upper East Side flagship. Attention to detail and immaculate service are mere foreplay, as the real brilliance comes with such inspired culinary creations as black truffle-layered sea scallops in puff pastry, morels with duck and foie gras stuffing, and roasted tuna with country bacon, chanterelles and truffled beef jus. With more than 1,500 wine labels to choose from and a two-page dessert menu, one side devoted entirely to chocolate, love may not be a strong enough word to describe New York's long-term affair with this most exquisite restaurant. Jacket required and tie suggested. Full bar. Serving dinner Mon–Sat. Closed Sun.

Michelin Guide: ★★ (excellent cooking and worth a detour)
The New York Times: ★★★★ (extraordinary); Top Pick
New York magazine: ★★★★ (exceptional, consistently
  elite); Critics' Pick
Zagat: 28 food rating (extraordinary to perfection)
Time Out New York: Critics' Pick

89

davidburke & donatella

133 E 61st St (bet Park and Lexington Aves)
New York, NY 10065
(212) 813-2121

Neighborhood Map: **Upper East Side**
Categories: **Brunch, Contemporary**
Price Range: **$$$**
www.dbdrestaurant.com

Though David Burke and Donatella Arpaia have parted ways, the show goes on. Burke has stayed with the restaurant, which faces an imminent name change. Diners still will find contemporary American food here, served so artfully — with a bit of high-brow funk, even — that the path from kitchen to table can seem a little like a culinary fashion runway. Full bar. Serving lunch Mon–Fri, dinner nightly. Sat–Sun brunch.

The New York Times: ★★ (very good); Top Pick

New York magazine: ★★★ (generally excellent); Critics' Pick
Zagat: 25 food rating (very good to excellent)
Time Out New York: Critics' Pick

Dawat

210 E 58th St (near 3rd Ave)
New York, NY 10022
(212) 355-7555

Neighborhood Map: **Midtown East/Murray Hill**
Category: **Indian**
Price Range: **$$**
www.restaurant.com/microsite.asp?rid=301000

Dawat characterizes its range of Indian cuisine, served in a posh dining room, as everything from "Bombay street fare and home-style tandoor cooking" to the kind of refined foods enjoyed by "the royal families." Three-, four- and five-course prix fixe menus available. Reservations required. Full bar. Serving lunch Mon–Sat, dinner nightly.

The New York Times: ★ (good)
Zagat: 23 food rating (very good to excellent)

DB Bistro Moderne

★ **BEST BISTRO IN MIDTOWN WEST/THEATER DISTRICT**

55 W 44th St (bet 5th and 6th Aves)
New York, NY 10036
(212) 391-2400

Neighborhood Map: **Midtown West/Theater District**
Categories: **Bistro, Burgers, French**
Price Range: **$$$**
www.danielnyc.com

Home to the famous foie gras and black truffle burger, DB Bistro Moderne also houses other similarly delicious French bistro favorites. Reservations suggested. Full bar. Serving breakfast and dinner daily, lunch Mon–Fri.

The New York Times: Top Pick
New York magazine: ★★ (very good); Critics' Pick
Zagat: 25 food rating (very good to excellent)
Time Out New York: Critics' Pick

Defonte's

★ **BEST SUBS/HOAGIES/PO-BOYS IN BROOKLYN**

379 Columbia St (near Luquer St)
Brooklyn, NY 11231
(718) 625-8052

Neighborhood Map: **Brooklyn (Red Hook)**
Category: **Subs/Hoagies/Po-boys**
Price Range: **$**

It's well worth a trip to Red Hook to sample these delectable, classic Italian heroes. No alcohol available. Cash only. Serving during breakfast and lunch hours Mon–Sat. Closed Sun.

New York magazine: Critics' Pick
The Village Voice: Critics' Pick

Degustation Wine & Tasting Bar

★ **BEST SMALL PLATES IN THE EAST VILLAGE/NOHO**

239 E 5th St (near 2nd Ave)
New York, NY 10003
(212) 979-1012

91

Neighborhood Map: **East Village/NoHo**
Categories: **French, Small Plates, Spanish, Wine Bar**
Price Range: **$$**

Locals crowd around the tasting bar at Degustation, a grazer's paradise and the latest venture from restaurateurs Jack and Grace Lamb, whose names sound like characters in a children's book. These tapas are for grown-up appetites, though, with a featured five-course tasting menu. Beer and wine available. Serving dinner Mon–Sat. Closed Sun.

The New York Times: ★★ (very good)
New York magazine: Critics' Pick
Zagat: 27 food rating (extraordinary to perfection)
Time Out New York: Critics' Pick
The Village Voice: Critics' Pick

NEW YORK CITY ★TOP100 **Del Posto**

★ **BEST ITALIAN IN CHELSEA**

85 10th Ave (bet 15th and 16th Sts)
New York, NY 10011
(212) 497-8090

Neighborhood Map: **Chelsea**
Categories: **Italian, Wine Bar**
Price Range: **$$$$**
www.delposto.com

With TV shows, cookbooks and restaurants spanning the
country between the three of them, Joseph Bastianich, Lidia
Bastianich and Mario Batali, who partnered to found Del Posto
in 2005, have become the Super Friends of the restaurant
scene. Batali fanatics, leave your Crocs at the door this time:
The ultra-luxurious décor demands more formal shoes, starkly
contrasting Batali's more accessible ventures (Babbo, Lupa).
No indulgence is spared, with marble in abundance, an elegant
staircase leading to dramatic balcony seating, music from a
baby grand piano, and even valet parking. The food matches the
backdrop in ambition, as classic Italian meets a contemporary
approach elevated with French fussiness. Pastas headlining
the menu include sheep's milk ricotta *gnudi* and risotto for
two with Dungeness crab, jalapeño and minced scallion. Meats
and fish are often portioned for two as well and sometimes
are carved at the table. Worthy options include wood-grilled
lobster, grilled squab and the Dover sole (for two) with summer
vegetable Scafata and salsa *verde*. Despite the fancy digs and
fine china, you'll still find Batali's beloved *lardo* (yes, pork fat)
for spreading on focaccia. The wine bar offers a slightly less
theatrical, and less costly, dining experience. Reservations
suggested. Full bar. Serving lunch Wed–Fri, dinner nightly.

Michelin Guide: ★★ (excellent cooking and worth a detour)
The New York Times: ★★★ (excellent); Top Pick
New York magazine: ★★★ (generally excellent); Critics' Pick
Zagat: 26 food rating (extraordinary to perfection)
The Village Voice: Critics' Pick

Dessert Truck

Neighborhood Map: **East Village/NoHo (nighttime location)**
St. Marks Pl at 3rd Ave
New York, NY 10003
no telephone

Neighborhood Map: **Midtown East/Murray Hill (daytime
location)**

92

Park Ave bet 51st and 53rd Sts
New York, NY 10022
no telephone

Category: **Dessert**
Price Range: **$**
www.desserttruck.com

A mobile dessert operation serving restaurant quality (or
better) desserts. No alcohol available. Cash only. Serving
from noon–5 pm Mon–Fri at Midtown location. Serving from 6
pm–midnight nightly at East Village location.

NEW YORK CITY
★TOP100 **Di Fara Pizza**

★ **BEST PIZZA IN NYC**
1424 Ave J (near E 15th St)
Brooklyn, NY 11230
(718) 258-1367

Neighborhood Map: **Brooklyn (Midwood)**
Categories: **Italian, Pizza**
Price Range: **$$**

93

With the exception of former patrons who resent its popularity
and one particularly cantankerous Gothamist reviewer, Di Fara
in Brooklyn's Midwood is pretty much universally beloved for its
outstanding, old-school pizzas. Domenico De Marco, who has
a cult following that rivals the Mario Batalis and Bobby Flays of
the world, meticulously crafts every pie sold. Yes, this means
a long wait, but consider it a rite of passage, or a chance to
get hungry. Sure, the place is not much to look at, with green
walls, fluorescent lighting, a few ceiling fans (in lieu of AC)
and countless framed awards, but the freshly made dough and
herbs grown in-house are the more important amenities to
consider. Many purists argue that toppings detract from the
simple brilliance of De Marco's pizzas, but they prove hard to
resist when they're this good. Thick-sliced, flavorful pepperoni,
porcini mushrooms and artichokes perfectly complement the
copious amounts of olive oil, fresh mozzarella and crispy crust.
The fresh basil, added as soon as the pies come out of the oven,
is a difference-maker as well. Note that Di Fara is sometimes
closed from about 4:30 pm–5:30 pm, when Mr. De Marco takes a
nap. Every genius needs his sleep. No alcohol available. BYOB.
Cash only. Serving lunch and dinner Tue–Sun. Closed Mon.

The New York Times: Top Pick
New York magazine: Critics' Pick
Zagat: 27 food rating (extraordinary to perfection)

★TOP100 Diner

★ BEST BRUNCH IN BROOKLYN

85 Broadway (near Berry St)
Brooklyn, NY 11211
(718) 486-3077

Neighborhood Map: **Brooklyn (Williamsburg)**
Categories: **Brunch, Contemporary**
Price Range: **$$**
www.dinernyc.com

Unlike most foodies who happily travel outside of their respective provincial culinary boundaries in pursuit of great eats, friends Mark Firth and Andrew Tarlow decided to launch their own joint within walking distance of their Williamsburg residence. Diner opened on New Year's Eve in 1998 in a converted 1920s dining car with chef Caroline Fidanza preparing the upscale-casual favorites that have henceforth kept this local haunt thumping. The greasy-spoon-turned-trendy-hipster-hangout fuels the neighborhood clientele with staples of burgers and goat cheese salads, but all kinds of people are willing to venture down to the South Side for the mouthwatering portions of specials such as roasted beet risotto or braised duck and white bean stew. Full bar. Serving lunch Mon–Fri, dinner and late-night nightly. Sat–Sun brunch 11 am–4pm.

New York magazine: Critics' Pick
Zagat: 21 food rating (very good to excellent)
Time Out New York: Critics' Pick

Dinosaur Bar-B-Que

★ BEST BARBECUE IN HARLEM

646 W 131st St (bet Broadway and 12th Ave)
New York, NY 10027
(212) 694-1777

Neighborhood Map: **Harlem**
Category: **Barbecue**
Price Range: **$$**

94

www.dinosaurbarbque.com

Since opening in 2004, this wildly popular spot in Harlem has wowed the crowds with ribs, pulled pork, brisket and blues. Full bar. Serving lunch, dinner and late-night daily.

New York magazine: Critics' Pick
Zagat: 22 food rating (very good to excellent)

Donguri

309 E 83rd St (bet 1st and 2nd Aves)
New York, NY 10028
(212) 737-5656

Neighborhood Map: **Upper East Side**
Category: **Japanese/Sushi**
Price Range: **$$$**
www.itoen.com/donguri

A hidden gem on the Upper East Side for deliciously authentic Japanese dishes. Beer, wine and sake available. Serving dinner Tue–Sun. Closed Mon.

95

The New York Times: ★★ (very good); Top Pick
Zagat: 27 food rating (extraordinary to perfection)

Dovetail

★ **BEST CONTEMPORARY ON THE UPPER WEST SIDE**
103 W 77th St (near Columbus Ave)
New York, NY 10024
(212) 362-3800

Neighborhood Map: **Upper West Side**
Category: **Contemporary**
Price Range: **$$$**
www.dovetailnyc.com

A hop, skip and a jump (or just one dinosaur step) from the Museum of Natural History, chef/owner John Fraser's Dovetail is one of the most celebrated of the newer restaurants in the city. Reservations suggested. Full bar. Serving dinner nightly.

The New York Times: ★★★ (excellent)

New York magazine: ★★★ (generally excellent); Critics' Pick
Zagat: 26 food rating (extraordinary to perfection)
Time Out New York: Critics' Pick

Doyers Vietnamese

11 Doyers St (bet Pell and Bowery Sts)
New York, NY 10013
(212) 513-1521

Neighborhood Map: **Chinatown**
Category: **Vietnamese**
Price Range: **$**

Tucked away in a Chinatown alley, Doyers will make your
search worthwhile with Vietnamese fare that's a cut above the
rest in the area. Beer and wine available. Serving lunch and
dinner daily.

Zagat: 21 food rating (very good to excellent)

DuMont

★ BEST BURGERS IN BROOKLYN

432 Union Ave (near Metropolitan Ave)
Brooklyn, NY 11211
(718) 486-7717

Neighborhood Map: **Brooklyn (Williamsburg)**
Categories: **American Traditional, Brunch, Burgers**
Price Range: **$$**
www.dumontrestaurant.com

A splendid burger, a beautiful patio out back and an inviting
ambiance make DuMont one of the best bets in Williamsburg.
Full bar. Serving lunch Mon–Fri, dinner Mon–Sat, late-night
Fri–Sat. Sat–Sun brunch 11 am–3 pm.

The New York Times: Top Pick
New York magazine: Critics' Pick
Zagat: 24 food rating (very good to excellent)

Dumpling House

★ BEST DUMPLINGS ON THE LOWER EAST SIDE

118 Eldridge St (near Broome St)
New York, NY 10002
(212) 625-8008

Neighborhood Map: **Lower East Side**
Categories: **Chinese, Dumplings**
Price Range: **$**

As its name suggests, the currency here are hand-made,
flavor-filled dumplings (some say the best in the city) at
absurdly low prices. No alcohol available. Cash only. Serving
breakfast, lunch and dinner daily.

New York magazine: Critics' Pick
Time Out New York: Critics' Pick

Dumpling Man

★ BEST DUMPLINGS IN THE EAST VILLAGE/NOHO
100 St Marks Pl (near 1st Ave)
New York, NY 10009
(212) 505-2121

Neighborhood Map: **East Village/NoHo**
Categories: **Chinese, Dumplings**
Price Range: **$**
www.dumplingman.com

97

Watch your north Asian-style dumplings being delicately crafted
before your eyes at this narrow little hole in the wall near First
Avenue. With low prices, frozen dumplings available for purchase,
delivery service and an undeniably cute logo, do we smell an
international dumpling chain empire in the future? Beer available.
Serving lunch and dinner daily, late-night Fri–Sun.

New York magazine: Critics' Pick
Zagat: 18 food rating (good to very good)

Eatery

★ BEST BRUNCH IN MIDTOWN WEST/THEATER DISTRICT
798 9th Ave (near 53rd St)
New York, NY 10019
(212) 765-7080

Neighborhood Map: **Midtown West/Theater District**

Categories: **American Traditional, Brunch, Contemporary**
Price Range: **$$**
www.eaterynyc.com

Eatery, or E-bar, as it's known by the trendy younger crowd that dines within, serves a popular, affordable Sunday brunch to Hell's Kitchen and beyond. This chic spot brings modern (and sometimes global) twists to home-style favorites, such as mac and cheese with frizzled onions. Full bar. Serving lunch Mon–Fri, dinner nightly, late-night Tue–Sat. Sat–Sun brunch 9 am–3:45 pm.

Zagat: 19 food rating (good to very good)

Egg

★ **BEST BREAKFAST IN BROOKLYN**

135 N 5th St (near Bedford Ave)
Brooklyn, NY 11211
(718) 302-5151

Neighborhood Map: **Brooklyn (Williamsburg)**
Categories: **American Traditional, Breakfast, Brunch**
Price Range: **$$**

Sign your name on the giant notepad out front, and wait your turn to be seated. After sampling Brooklyn's best breakfast (make sure you try the biscuits), you'll be glad you did. No alcohol available. Serving breakfast, lunch and dinner daily.

New York magazine: Critics' Pick
Zagat: 24 food rating (very good to excellent)

Eight Mile Creek

240 Mulberry St (near Prince St)
New York, NY 10012
(212) 431-4635

Neighborhood Map: **Little Italy/NoLita**
Categories: **Australian, Brunch, Contemporary**
Price Range: **$$**
www.eightmilecreek.com

Real Australian beers, contemporary cuisine and lively environs make for a memorable evening at this restaurant founded by three native Aussies. Kangaroo skewers are on the menu (and worth a try), but this spot is thankfully devoid of koala bears, boomerangs and fried onion appetizers. Reservations suggested. Full bar. Serving dinner and late-night nightly. Sat–Sun brunch starting 11 am.

The New York Times: ★★ (very good); Top Pick
Zagat: 20 food rating (very good to excellent)

Eisenberg's Sandwich Shop

174 5th Ave (bet 22nd and 23rd Sts)
New York, NY 10010
(212) 675-5096

Neighborhood Map: **Union Square/Flatiron**
Categories: **Breakfast, Burgers, Diner**
Price Range: **$**
www.eisenbergsnyc.com

Step back in time with breakfast, lunch or early dinner at this real-deal luncheonette open since 1929. No alcohol available. Serving breakfast and lunch Mon–Sat. Closed Sun.

The Village Voice: Critics' Pick

99

EJ's Luncheonette

★ BEST DINER ON THE UPPER EAST SIDE
Neighborhood Map: **Upper East Side**
1271 3rd Ave (near 73rd St)
New York, NY 10021
(212) 472-0600

★ BEST DINER ON THE UPPER WEST SIDE
Neighborhood Map: **Upper West Side**
447 Amsterdam Ave (bet 81st and 82nd Sts)
New York, NY 10024
(212) 873-3444

Categories: **American Traditional, Breakfast, Brunch, Diner**
Price Range: **$$**

Known for being particularly family-friendly (the kids' menu includes hot dogs, grilled cheese, PB&J and so forth), the

grown-ups come here for the popular brunch menu. Beer and wine available. Cash only. Serving lunch and dinner daily. West side location also serving breakfast daily. Sat–Sun brunch. Hours vary by locations.

Zagat: 16 food rating (good to very good)

NEW YORK CITY
★TOP100 Eleven Madison Park

★ **BEST CONTEMPORARY IN GRAMERCY/MADISON PARK**

11 Madison Ave (near 24th St)
New York, NY 10010
(212) 889-0905

Neighborhood Map: **Gramercy/Madison Park**
Categories: **Contemporary, French**
Price Range: **$$$$$**
www.elevenmadisonpark.com

An integral part of Danny Meyer's ever expanding restaurant empire (Gramercy Tavern, Union Square Cafe, Tabla et al.), Eleven Madison Park is quintessential Gotham. Marble floors, impossibly high ceilings, elegant wrought-iron chandeliers and tall windows overlooking the park distinguish this art deco dining room that was once a bank. The visually striking Gramercy restaurant has revamped and gained serious momentum since James Beard award-nominated chef Daniel Humm took the helm in 2006. Colorful and aesthetically intriguing food presentations and reputably unpretentious and helpful service render EMP a crowd favorite and dining destination for out-of-towners. Humm has taken the progressive cuisine in a more French direction, and indulgent menu standouts include foie gras, Vermont suckling pig, Muscovy duck for two with lavender honey, and Black Angus beef tenderloin with Bordelaise sauce. Diners can choose a three-course prix fixe meal or opt for the tasting menu with optional wine pairings. While you're splurging, you might as well kick back with a Monkey Gland (gin, absinthe, grenadine, orange juice) or a Mississippi Buck (bourbon, ginger-infused lime syrup and soda). Reservations suggested. Full bar with award-winning wine list. Serving lunch Mon–Fri, dinner Mon–Sat. Closed Sun.

The New York Times: ★★★ (excellent); Top Pick
New York magazine: ★★★ (generally excellent); Critics' Pick
Zagat: 27 food rating (extraordinary to perfection)

Epistrophy

★ **BEST WINE BAR IN LITTLE ITALY/NOLITA**

200 Mott St (bet Kenmare and Spring Sts)
New York, NY 10012
(212) 966-0904

Neighborhood Map: **Little Italy/NoLita**
Categories: **Café, Italian, Wine Bar**
Price Range: **$$**
www.epistrophycafe.com

A funky little NoLita wine bar with a sea green storefront,
Epistrophy serves cheese plates, espresso, panini and reasonably
priced wines to a hip clientele. Beer and wine available. Cash
only. Serving during lunch, dinner and late-night daily.

Erminia

250 E 83rd St (bet 2nd and 3rd Aves)
New York, NY 10028
(212) 879-4284

Neighborhood Map: **Upper East Side**
Category: **Italian**
Price Range: **$$$**

101

This very small, very romantic Upper East Side Italian
restaurant will leave you absolutely enchanted. Beer and wine
available. Serving dinner Mon–Sat. Closed Sun.

Zagat: 25 food rating (very good to excellent)

NEW YORK CITY
★TOP100 Esca

★ **BEST ITALIAN IN MIDTOWN WEST/THEATER DISTRICT**

402 W 43rd St (near 9th Ave)
New York, NY 10036
(212) 564-7272

Neighborhood Map: **Midtown West/Theater District**
Categories: **Italian, Seafood**
Price Range: **$$$**
www.esca-nyc.com

Another creation of television icon/restaurant baron Mario

Batali (along with partner Joseph Bastianich and chef David Pasternack), Esca is fundamentally a fish restaurant focused on coastal Italian-style preparation. The calling card of this theater-district favorite, opened in 2000, is the freshest fish available — "the most sought after Pacific Ocean delicacies alongside fluke that Dave caught on his day off," boasts Esca's website. The culinary theme extends to the wine list, which is exclusively Italian. (But if you're looking for Chianti or pinot grigio, you'll be *senza fortuna*.) And the constantly changing menu includes *crudo*, Italian for raw fish, which is available for whole-table tastings of two flights per person. If an anti-piscine diner somehow passes through the doors, there are always the gnocchi with wild mushrooms, ravioli with braised baby lamb or the roasted local wild duck with lentils and balsamic cippoline. (But look out for that birdshot!) Reservations suggested. Full bar. Serving lunch Mon–Sat, dinner nightly.

The New York Times: ★★★ (excellent); Top Pick
New York magazine: ★★★ (generally excellent); Critics' Pick
Zagat: 25 food rating (very good to excellent)
Time Out New York: Critics' Pick

NEW YORK CITY
⭐**TOP100** **Ess-a-Bagel**

★ **BEST BAGELS IN NYC**
Neighborhood Map: **Gramercy/Madison Park**
359 1st Ave (near 21st St)
New York, NY 10010
(212) 260-2252

Neighborhood Map: **Midtown East/Murray Hill**
831 3rd Ave (bet 50th and 51st Sts)
New York, NY 10022
(212) 980-1010

Categories: **Bagels, Breakfast, Deli**
Price Range: **$**
www.ess-a-bagel.com

"Everything on a bagel" is the motto of this landmark First Avenue bagel shop, opened in 1976, and its sister Third Avenue location in Midtown Manhattan. Its founders come from Austrian baking stock and know their way around bagels, producing so many hand-rolled versions of this consummate comfort food every day that regulars are accustomed to being mildly assaulted by the baking heat when they enter the door. For a beloved bagel joint, the menu is extensive, offering salad platters, soups, various knishes, side items and a variety of chicken, meat and fish sandwiches — including lox and cream cheese, of course. Among other endearing traits, Ess-a-Bagel is known for its bounteous portions of cream cheese, which *The Village Voice* once drooled, "comes in big, gobby layers, oozing out the center." That's the best kind. No alcohol available. Serving during breakfast, lunch and dinner daily.

Zagat: 23 food rating (very good to excellent)

NEW YORK CITY
★TOP100 **Estiatorio Milos**

★ **BEST GREEK IN NYC**
125 W 55th St (bet 6th and 7th Aves)
New York, NY 10019
(212) 245-7400

Neighborhood Map: **Midtown West/Theater District**
Categories: **Greek, Seafood**
Price Range: **$$$$**
www.milos.ca

If New York were Mount Olympus, Estiatorio Milos would be the Zeus of divine Mediterranean seafood restaurants, reigning proudly over lesser deities. Greek expatriate Costas Spiliadis launched his massive, elegant Midtown Manhattan space in 1997, having opened his first Milos in Montreal two decades prior, to the fervent "oopahs" of New York foodies eager to benefit from Spiliadis' intimate relationships with boutique fisheries across the globe. Priced-by-the-pound fish and tentacled delicacies shine like the Golden Fleece from iced display cases, tempting diners with choices from Icelandic Arctic char to Floridian swordfish. Each catch's pure preparation using only lemon, olive oil and herbs — granted any garnish from honey to caper is specially imported from the world's most reputed distributors — transports diners to a small, nameless village in the Cyclades, where life hangs on the enjoyment of each celestial bite. Reservations suggested. Full bar. Serving lunch Mon–Fri, dinner nightly.

The New York Times: ★★ (very good); Top Pick
New York magazine: Critics' Pick
Zagat: 27 food rating (extraordinary to perfection)
Time Out New York: Critics' Pick

THE BEST RESTAURANTS

★TOP100 NEW YORK CITY Etats-Unis

242 E 81st St (bet 2nd and 3rd Aves)
New York, NY 10028
(212) 517-8826

Neighborhood Map: **Upper East Side**
Categories: **Bistro, Contemporary**
Price Range: **$$$**
www.etatsunisrestaurant.com

Viva New York, a city where memorable dining treasures
often exist across the street from where the limelight
touches down. Such is the case with the Upper East Side's
Etats-Unis: Just opposite the first-rate, Michelin-starred,
line-out-the-door main restaurant, locals also head to the
satellite Bar@Etats-Unis, which has its own unique character
but serves the same nightly changing menu, as well as a few
more rustic choices. Either spot offers a pleasantly intimate
atmosphere to accompany an eclectic bistro menu of spot-on
contemporary creations, such as steamed lobster salad or
Niman Ranch pork shoulder braised in onions, poblanos and
citrus juice. Top it all off with some delectable date pudding
and a choice from the outstanding wine list. Full bar. Main
restaurant serving dinner nightly. Bar@Etats-Unis serving
lunch Mon–Sat, dinner nightly.

Michelin Guide: ★ (a very good restaurant in its category)
The New York Times: ★★ (very good); Top Pick
New York magazine: Critics' Pick
Zagat: 24 food rating (very good to excellent)
Time Out New York: Critics' Pick

Faicco's

Neighborhood Map: **Brooklyn (Dyker Heights)**
6511 11th Ave (near 65th St)
Brooklyn, NY 11219
(718) 236-0119

★ BEST SUBS/HOAGIES/PO-BOYS IN THE WEST VILLAGE/ MEATPACKING DISTRICT

Neighborhood Map: **West Village/Meatpacking District**
260 Bleecker St (bet Cornelia and Morton Sts)
New York, NY 10014
(212) 243-1974

Categories: **Deli, Gourmet Takeout, Subs/Hoagies/
Po-boys**
Price Range: **$**

Part gourmet grocery and part Italian sandwich mecca, Faicco's
makes the best heros around. No alcohol available. Serving
during breakfast and lunch hours Tue–Sun, early dinner hours
Tue–Sat. Closed Mon.

The Village Voice: Critics' Pick

NEW YORK CITY ★**TOP100** Falai

68 Clinton St (bet Rivington and Stanton Sts)
New York, NY 10002
(212) 253-1960

Neighborhood Map: **Lower East Side**
Category: **Italian**
Price Range: **$$$**
www.falainyc.com

105

White lights, white brick walls, white tables and white chairs
bedeck this white-hot dining room on the Lower East Side.
The shimmering space looks straight out of the future as
imagined by a 1970s sci-fi film. The beautiful room and beautiful
people who dine within are only part of the draw, though, as
it is chef Iacopo Falai's progressive Italian cuisine that keeps
the restaurant consistently busy. Its immense popularity has
inspired the owner to open more casual concepts, namely Falai
Panetteria and Caffe Falai. At the flagship restaurant, cheeses
abound, and inventive pastas such as spinach and ricotta *gnudi*
or green pea pappardelle with wild boar ragu are the norm. And
Iacopo Falai was the pastry chef at Le Cirque, so it'd be foolish
to miss the passion fruit soufflé or other dessert specials. In
season, the outdoor garden area provides a greener alternative
to the whiteness. Reservations suggested. Beer and wine
available. Serving dinner nightly.

The New York Times: ★★ (very good); Top Pick
New York magazine: ★★ (very good); Critics' Pick
Zagat: 24 food rating (very good to excellent)
Time Out New York: Critics' Pick
The Village Voice: Critics' Pick

Felidia

243 E 58th St (near 2nd Ave)
New York, NY 10022
(212) 758-1479

Neighborhood Map: **Midtown East/Murray Hill**
Category: **Italian**
Price Range: **$$$**
www.felidia-nyc.com

Another in TV personality/restaurateur Lidia Bastianich's quiver, Felidia serves up regional Italian delicacies via Italian chef Fortunato Nicotra in a bright, beautiful dining room and offers a three-course prix fixe lunch option. Reservations suggested. Full bar. Serving lunch Mon–Fri, dinner nightly.

The New York Times: ★★★ (excellent)
New York magazine: Critics' Pick
Zagat: 26 food rating (extraordinary to perfection)
Time Out New York: Critics' Pick

NEW YORK CITY
★TOP100 Fiamma

★ **BEST ITALIAN IN SOHO**

206 Spring St (bet Sullivan St and 6th Ave)
New York, NY 10012
(212) 653-0100

Neighborhood Map: **SoHo**
Category: **Italian**
Price Range: **$$$$$**
www.brguestrestaurants.com

SoHo's Fiamma embodies indulgence. A Steve Hanson (Dos Caminos, Atlantic Grill) production, this two-tiered, town house restaurant recruited James Beard award-winning chef Fabio Trabocchi in 2007. And Trabocchi (most recently of Maestro outside D.C.) has not disappointed, wowing critics, special-occasion diners and the Wall Street elite with Italian-rooted fare. Grab a mint julep or a Juno (vodka, strawberry, rhubarb, tonic) from the bar, and ... Ready. Set. Decadence! Prix fixe meals (no á la carte available) come in three-, five- or seven-course tasting menus. First courses may include Hudson Valley foie gras with peaches and opal basil, or the duo of Wagyu beef carpaccio and tartare. Ravioli of sheep's milk ricotta and tagliolini with lamb ragu are among house-made pastas. Grimaud Farms duck and roasted veal loin with celery root purée round out the menu. Reservations suggested. Full bar. Serving dinner Mon–Sat. Late-night Fri–Sat. Closed Sun.

Michelin Guide: ★ (a very good restaurant in its category)
The New York Times: ★★★ (excellent); Top Pick
New York magazine: ★★ (very good); Critics' Pick
Zagat: 24 food rating (very good to excellent)

Five Front

5 Front St (near Old Fulton St)
Brooklyn, NY 11201
(718) 625-5559

Neighborhood Map: **Brooklyn (Dumbo)**
Categories: **American Traditional, Brunch, Contemporary**
Price Range: **$$**
www.fivefrontrestaurant.com

Contemporary dishes are served in an Old World setting right on the waterfront in Dumbo. Reservations suggested. Full bar. Serving dinner Wed–Mon. Sat–Sun brunch. Closed Tue.

New York magazine: Critics' Pick
Zagat: 20 food rating (very good to excellent)
Time Out New York: Critics' Pick

Fleur de Sel

5 E 20th St (bet 5th Ave and Broadway)
New York, NY 10003
(212) 460-9100

Neighborhood Map: **Union Square/Flatiron**
Category: **French**
Price Range: **$$$$$**
www.fleurdeselnyc.com

The quaint, exposed-brick interior at Fleur de Sel fits nicely with the sophisticated cuisine influenced by the flavors of Brittany. Reservations suggested. Full bar. Serving lunch and dinner daily.

107

Michelin Guide: ★ (a very good restaurant in its category)
The New York Times: ★★ (very good)
New York magazine: ★★ (very good); Critics' Pick
Zagat: 25 food rating (very good to excellent)
Time Out New York: Critics' Pick

Food Sing 88 Corp.

2 E Broadway (near Bowery St)
New York, NY 10038
(212) 219-8223

Neighborhood Map: **Chinatown**
Categories: **Chinese, Noodle House**
Price Range: **$**

Known for its long wheat noodles and nourishing broths, Food
Sing 88 keeps noodles grounded, affordable and delicious despite
the recent proliferation of trendier noodle houses. Cash only. No
alcohol available. Serving breakfast, lunch and dinner daily.

The Village Voice: Critics' Pick

108

NEW YORK CITY
★TOP100 The Four Seasons

★ **BEST CONTINENTAL IN NYC**
99 E 52nd St (bet Park and Lexington Aves)
New York, NY 10022
(212) 754-9494

Neighborhood Map: **Midtown East/Murray Hill**
Categories: **Contemporary, Continental**
Price Range: **$$$$**
www.fourseasonsrestaurant.com

If ever a single space were to live and breathe Manhattan, The
Four Seasons is it. Dine in Trump or Bloomberg's shoes at one of
America's most iconic eateries. GPS coordinates for New York's
anointed power-lunch posse lie somewhere inside the walls of
the Grill Room — the location of JFK's 45th birthday party —
while the elegant Pool Room hosts many a polished pair seeking
the indubitably magical experience of dining in Manhattan's only
restaurant designated an official landmark. Though perhaps not
on the forefront of progressive Continental cuisine, the kitchen
shines with the classics: Châteaubriand, rack of lamb and Dover

sole. Jacket required. Reservations suggested. Full bar. Serving lunch Mon–Fri, dinner Mon–Sat. Closed Sun.

The New York Times: ★★ (very good)
New York magazine: ★★ (very good); Critics' Pick
Zagat: 26 food rating (extraordinary to perfection)

Frankies 17 Spuntino/Frankies 457 Spuntino

★ BEST ITALIAN ON THE LOWER EAST SIDE

Neighborhood Map: **Lower East Side**
17 Clinton St (near Stanton St)
New York, NY 10022
(212) 253-2303

Neighborhood Map: **Brooklyn (Carroll Gardens)**
457 Court St (near 4th Pl)
Brooklyn, NY 11231
(718) 403-0033

Categories: **Brunch, Italian**
Price Range: **$$**
www.frankiesspuntino.com

109

Exquisitely prepared Italian dishes in a casual but beautiful setting. The cavatelli with Faicco's hot sausage is simply to die for. Full bar at Brooklyn location. Beer and wine available at Lower East Side location. Cash only. Serving lunch and dinner daily. Late-night hours vary by location. Sat–Sun brunch.

New York magazine: Critics' Pick
Zagat: 24 food rating (very good to excellent)

Franny's

295 Flatbush Ave (near Prospect Pl)
Brooklyn, NY 11217
(718) 230-0221

Neighborhood Map: **Brooklyn (Park Slope)**
Categories: **Italian, Pizza**
Price Range: **$$**
www.frannysbrooklyn.com

Gourmet pizzas made from locally sourced ingredients are only a part of what makes Franny's so delicious. A great twist on the classic New York pizzeria. Full bar. Serving lunch Sat–Sun, dinner nightly.

The New York Times: ★★ (very good); Top Pick
New York magazine: ★ (good); Critics' Pick
Zagat: 25 food rating (very good to excellent)
Time Out New York: Critics' Pick
The Village Voice: Critics' Pick

Fuleen Seafood

11 Division St (bet Bowery St and E Broadway)
New York, NY 10002
(212) 941-6888

Neighborhood Map: **Chinatown**
Categories: **Chinese, Seafood**
Price Range: **$$**

A bounty of marine life greets you in the windows of Fuleen's Seafood before making the short trip from the tank to your table. Helpful servers will guide you through specialties from both land and sea. Beer, wine and sake available. Serving lunch, dinner and late-night daily.

Zagat: 23 food rating (very good to excellent)

Gabriel's Bar & Restaurant

11 W 60th St (near Broadway)
New York, NY 10023
(212) 956-4600

Neighborhood Map: **Upper West Side**
Category: **Italian**
Price Range: **$$$**
www.gabrielsbarandrest.com

Popular for the business lunch crowd by day and for pre-theater meals at night, Gabriel's, located near Lincoln Center, features northern Italian-inspired fine dining. Full bar. Serving lunch Mon–Fri, dinner Mon–Sat. Closed Sun.

The New York Times: ★★ (very good)
Zagat: 22 food rating (very good to excellent)

Gahm Mi Oak

43 W 32nd St (bet Broadway and 5th Ave)
New York, NY 10001
(212) 695-4113

Neighborhood Map: **Garment District**
Category: **Korean**
Price Range: **$$**

In the heart of bustling Koreatown, Gahm Mi Oak stays
open 24/7 and is known for its mythical, hangover-curing
sul long tang soup. Beer, wine and sake available. Open 24
hours.

Zagat: 20 food rating (very good to excellent)

Garden Cafe

620 Vanderbilt Ave (near Prospect Pl)
Brooklyn, NY 11238
(718) 857-8863

Neighborhood Map: **Brooklyn (Prospect Heights)**
Category: **Contemporary**
Price Range: **$$**

The epitome of a hidden gem, this lovely and intimate
Prospect Heights eatery serves superb contemporary fare to
crowds of locals for dinner. The perfect spot for a special
occasion. Reservations suggested. Beer and wine available.
Serving dinner Tue–Sat. Closed Sun–Mon.

The New York Times: Top Pick
Zagat: 28 food rating (extraordinary to perfection)

Gennaro

665 Amsterdam Ave (bet 92nd and 93rd Sts)
New York, NY 10025
(212) 665-5348

Neighborhood Map: **Upper West Side**

111

Category: **Italian**
Price Range: **$$**

This casual and popular neighborhood Italian restaurant is family-friendly, traffics in fresh gnocchi and, best of all, is heavy on flavor but light on the wallet. Beer and wine available. Cash only. Serving dinner nightly.

The New York Times: Top Pick
New York magazine: ★ (good); Critics' Pick
Zagat: 24 food rating (very good to excellent)

NEW YORK CITY
★TOP100 Ghenet

★ **BEST AFRICAN IN NYC**
Neighborhood Map: **Brooklyn (Park Slope)**
348 Douglass St (near 4th Ave)
Brooklyn, NY 11217
(718) 230-4475

Neighborhood Map: **Little Italy/NoLita**
284 Mulberry St (bet Houston and Prince Sts)
New York, NY 10012
(212) 343-1888

Categories: **African, Vegetarian**
Price Range: **$$**
www.ghenet.com

Ditch your silverware and use your hands at NoLita's popular Ethiopian restaurant that's off the beaten path. This family-owned and -operated dining room is warm and welcoming, with bright red walls adorned with mirrors and paintings from local artists. A good place to get acquainted with the cuisine, Ghenet provides spongy *injera* bread in lieu of traditional utensils for picking up food. Dishes are served family-style, so sharing is encouraged. Entrées include the *doro wett* (seasoned chicken), *kitfo* (finely chopped beef served raw) or the *kelil merek*, a lamb stew. Ghenet also features 10 or so exclusively vegetarian entrées. A second location opened in Park Slope in early 2008. Reservations not accepted. Beer and wine available. Manhattan location serving lunch Tue–Sun, dinner nightly. Park Slope location serving dinner Tue–Sun. Closed Mon.

The New York Times: Top Pick
Zagat: 21 food rating (very good to excellent)

Giorgio's of Gramercy

★ **BEST AMERICAN TRADITIONAL IN UNION SQUARE/ FLATIRON**

27 E 21st St (bet Park Ave S and Broadway)
New York, NY 10010
(212) 477-0007

Neighborhood Map: **Union Square/Flatiron**
Category: **American Traditional**
Price Range: **$$**
www.giorgiosofgramercy.com

What you'll get here is the best of American cuisine with a few Italian dishes rounding out the menu. Reservations suggested. Full bar. Serving lunch Mon–Fri, dinner nightly.

Zagat: 21 food rating (very good to excellent)

The Good Fork

391 Van Brunt St (near Coffey St)
Brooklyn, NY 11231
(718) 643-6636

Neighborhood Map: **Brooklyn (Red Hook)**
Category: **Contemporary**
Price Range: **$$**
www.goodfork.com

Competition for some of the very best restaurants in Manhattan, The Good Fork provides Red Hook locals with positively heavenly Asian-inspired contemporary fare. Reservations suggested. Full bar. Serving dinner Tue–Sun. Closed Mon.

The New York Times: Top Pick
New York magazine: Critics' Pick
Zagat: 25 food rating (very good to excellent)

NEW YORK CITY ⭐**TOP100** **Gotham Bar and Grill**

12 E 12th St (bet 5th Ave and University Pl)
New York, NY 10003
(212) 620-4020

113

Neighborhood Map: **Greenwich Village**
Category: **Contemporary**
Price Range: **$$$$**
www.gothambarandgrill.com

Though vertical food may no longer be at the forefront of
cutting-edge cookery, chef Alfred Portale, who is largely
responsible for the movement, can still draw oohs and aahs
with his delightfully intriguing presentations and complex
flavors at one of New York's most revered restaurants.
Opened in 1984, Gotham Bar and Grill still packs them in with
its busy yet intimate atmosphere, world-class, unpretentious
service and absolute consistency. A prime spot for power
lunches or special-occasion dinners, the dining room is
distinguished by its soaring ceilings, floor-to-ceiling windows
and billowy white light fixtures. Lunch brings an affordable
three-course, prix fixe menu with optional wine pairings,
while monthly changing dinner menus feature first and second
courses such as black bass ceviche, Alaskan king crab risotto,
and the trademark seafood salad with scallops, octopus,
squid, lobster and avocado in a lemon vinaigrette. Dramatically
plated entrées may include juniper-spiced Muscovy duck
breast, porcini-crusted halibut, and roasted Maine lobster in
a red wine lobster reduction served with spaghetti squash,
potato purée and Brussels sprouts. Desserts are ambitious
and not to be missed, such as pastry chef Deborah Racicot's
pumpkin soufflé and signature apple cider beignets with Jack
Daniel's ice cream. Reservations suggested. Full bar with
extensive wine list. Serving lunch Mon–Fri, dinner nightly.

Michelin Guide: ★ (a very good restaurant in its category)
The New York Times: ★★★ (excellent); Top Pick
New York magazine: ★★★ (generally excellent); Critics' Pick
Zagat: 27 food rating (extraordinary to perfection)
Time Out New York: Critics' Pick

NEW YORK CITY
★TOP100 Gramercy Tavern
42 E 20th St (bet Broadway and Park Ave S)
New York, NY 10003
(212) 477-0777

Neighborhood Map: **Union Square/Flatiron**
Category: **Contemporary**
Price Range: **Dining Room $$$$$ Tavern $$**
www.gramercytavern.com

114

A Flatiron favorite for nearly 15 years now, Gramercy Tavern executes New American fine dining sans pretension, ambitious fusiony fare or gimmicky atmospheric touches. Instead, flowers, colorful murals and wood-beamed ceilings create a comfortable farmhouse ambiance. Since taking the reins from Tom Colicchio in 2006, chef Michael Anthony (formerly of Daniel and Blue Hill) has breathed new life into this rustic dining room with an aggressive farm-to-table approach — if you don't believe he means business about this slow-food philosophy, consider the five-course vegetable tasting menu. Though menus change seasonally, past prix fixe offerings in the main dining room have included pasture-raised roasted chicken with roasted and puréed carrots, smoked lobster, and rack of pork and braised belly. The less formal tavern up front features menu items á la carte at dinner. Reservations suggested. Full bar. Serving lunch Mon–Fri, dinner nightly. Tavern also serving late-night Fri–Sat.

Michelin Guide: ★ (a very good restaurant in its category)
The New York Times: ★★★ (excellent); Top Pick
New York magazine: ★★★ (generally excellent); Critics' Pick
Zagat: 28 food rating (extraordinary to perfection)
Time Out New York: Critics' Pick

NEW YORK CITY
★TOP100 Gray's Papaya

★ **BEST HOT DOGS IN NYC**
Neighborhood Map: **Garment District**
539 8th Ave (near 37th St)
New York, NY 10018
(212) 904-1588

Neighborhood Map: **Greenwich Village**
402 6th Ave (near 8th St)
New York, NY 10011
(212) 260-3532

Neighborhood Map: **Upper West Side**
2090 Broadway (near 72nd St)
New York, NY 10023
(212) 799-0243

Category: **Hot Dogs**
Price Range: **$**
www.grayspapaya.com

Sometimes, amid all the delicate veal sweetbreads, fall-off-the-bone braised short ribs and pan-seared sea scallops that Manhattan's fine-dining establishments have to offer, a New Yorker just needs a hot dog. For those times, there's Gray's Papaya, with three locations on the West Side. One perfectly grilled dog on a toasted bun: a buck and some change. A second frank and a non-alcoholic papaya drink: $3.50. Sinking your teeth into the otherwordly, all-beef, slightly crunchy casing: priceless. Cash only. No alcohol available. Open 24 hours.

Zagat: 21 food rating (very good to excellent)

The Grocery

288 Smith St (bet Union and Sackett Sts)
Brooklyn, NY 11231
(718) 596-3335

Neighborhood Map: **Brooklyn (Carroll Gardens)**
Category: **Contemporary**
Price Range: **$$$**
www.thegroceryrestaurant.com

Internationally inspired contemporary style and a charming setting put The Grocery at the top of the list of best eateries in restaurant-filled Carroll Gardens. Reservations suggested. Beer and wine available. Serving dinner Tue–Sat. Closed Sun–Mon.

The New York Times: ★ (good); Top Pick
New York magazine: ★ (good); Critics' Pick
Zagat: 27 food rating (extraordinary to perfection)
Time Out New York: Critics' Pick

Harry's Cafe and Steak

1 Hanover Sq (bet Pearl and Stone Sts)
New York, NY 10004
(212) 785-9200

Neighborhood Map: **Financial District**
Categories: **American Traditional, Steak House**
Price Range: **Steak House $$$$ Cafe $$$**
www.harrysnyc.com

116

A café on one side and an old-fashioned steak house on the other, Harry's is a great choice for a business lunch or dinner downtown. Reservations suggested. Full bar. Serving lunch, dinner and late-night daily.

The New York Times: ★ (good)
Zagat: 22 food rating (very good to excellent)

NEW YORK CITY
★TOP100 **Hatsuhana**

Neighborhood Map: **Midtown East/Murray Hill**
237 Park Ave (near 46th St)
New York, NY 10017
(212) 661-3400

Neighborhood Map: **Midtown East/Murray Hill**
17 E 48th St (bet 5th and Madison Aves)
New York, NY 10017
(212) 355-3345

Category: **Japanese/Sushi**
Price Range: **$$$**
www.hatsuhana.com

117

These two sushi stalwarts exposed many Midtown Manhattanites to the delicate art of sushi for the first time. Nowadays, sushi spots abound, often specializing in blaring house music, spicy mayonnaise-soaked, deep-fried rolls, and architecturally questionable stacked offerings. Hatsuhana takes a different approach by sticking to the *old* approach, claiming, "Sushi as a cuisine is conceptually simple. Ironically, its simplicity also makes it most complicated." The emphasis is on freshness and expert technique. The menu offers some basic sushi rolls and teriyaki and tempura dishes, but you'd probably be best served to leave your dinner up to the chef. There's the chef's sushi special (10 pieces), sashimi special (seven pieces) and the popular Box of Dreams, nine pieces of raw or cooked fish and sushi rice in a lacquer box. Both restaurants are popular for business lunches and for their artfully arranged takeout preparation as well. Reservations suggested. Full bar. Park Ave location serving lunch and dinner Mon–Fri. Closed Sat–Sun. 48th St location serving lunch and dinner Mon–Sat. Closed Sun.

The New York Times: ★★ (very good); Top Pick
New York magazine: Critics' Pick
Zagat: 24 food rating (very good to excellent)

Hearth

★ **BEST CONTEMPORARY IN THE EAST VILLAGE/NOHO**
403 E 12th St (near 1st Ave)
New York, NY 10009
(646) 602-1300

Neighborhood Map: **East Village/NoHo**
Category: **Contemporary**
Price Range: **$$$**
www.restauranthearth.com

Hestia (Greek goddess of the hearth and hospitality) would approve of the warm and welcoming vibe at this East Village contemporary restaurant, where the emphasis is on local and seasonal ingredients. Reservations suggested. Full bar. Serving dinner nightly.

The New York Times: ★★ (very good); Top Pick
New York magazine: ★★ (very good); Critics' Pick
Zagat: 25 food rating (very good to excellent)
Time Out New York: Critics' Pick

Hecho en Dumbo

111 Front St (near Washington St, Dumbo General Store)
Brooklyn, NY 11201
(718) 855-5288

Neighborhood Map: **Brooklyn (Dumbo)**
Category: **Mexican**
Price Range: **$$**
www.hechoendumbo.com

A celebration of Mexican food and culture in every way, Hecho en Dumbo prides itself on serving authentic dishes using the freshest ingredients available. Full bar. Cash only. Serving dinner Mon–Sat, late-night Thu–Sat.

New York magazine: Critics' Pick
Time Out New York: Critics' Pick

Henry's End

44 Henry St (near Cranberry St)
Brooklyn, NY 11201

(718) 834-1776

Neighborhood Map: **Brooklyn (Brooklyn Heights)**
Category: **American Traditional**
Price Range: **$$**
www.henrysend.com

A Brooklyn Heights staple, Henry's End features upscale
traditional American cuisine in a laid-back and comfortable
neighborhood setting. Meat lovers will find plenty to rave
about. Full bar. Serving dinner nightly.

Zagat: 24 food rating (very good to excellent)

NEW YORK CITY
★TOP100 Holy Basil

★ **BEST THAI IN NYC**
149 2nd Ave, 2nd Fl (bet 9th and 10th Sts)
New York, NY 10003
(212) 460-5557

Neighborhood Map: **East Village/NoHo**
Category: **Thai**
Price Range: **$$**
www.holybasilrestaurant.com

119

Though the name Holy Basil refers to a specific exotic species
of the herb said to counter physical, chemical and biological
stressors, most avid Thai food followers hold any kind of basil in
sacred regard because of its potent flavor and its contribution
to the cuisine. After eating at this East Village restaurant,
such enthusiasts for sweet and spicy accents will not leave
disappointed. Unlike your quaint neighborhood Thai kitchen, Holy
Basil establishes a decidedly romantic and elegant ambiance, with
very dark lighting, high ceilings, candles and lush red curtains.
Given the chic atmosphere, the low prices are a welcome
surprise. Start with a green papaya salad or steamed mussels in
a Thai-spiced white wine sauce. Curries are particularly popular,
such as Holy Basil's rendition of green curry or the shrimp and
scallops *panang* curry. And for heat seekers, there's always the
kee mao (rice noodles with holy basil leaves, chicken, shrimp and
chili pepper) or the very spicy *pet kaprow*, sliced crispy duck. Full
bar. Serving dinner nightly, late-night Fri–Sat.

The New York Times: Top Pick
Zagat: 21 food rating (very good to excellent)

Hummus Place

Neighborhood Map: **East Village/NoHo**
109 St. Marks Pl (near 1st Ave)
New York, NY 10009
(212) 529-9198

Neighborhood Map: **Greenwich Village**
99 Macdougal St (near Bleecker St)
New York, NY 10012
(212) 533-3089

Neighborhood Map: **Greenwich Village**
71 7th Ave S (bet Barrow and Bleecker Sts)
New York, NY 10014
(212) 924-2022

Neighborhood Map: **Upper West Side**
305 Amsterdam Ave (bet 74th and 75th Sts)
New York, NY 10023
(212) 799-3335

Categories: **Middle Eastern, Vegetarian**
Price Range: **$**
www.hummusplace.com

120

With four locations in the city, this unassuming and
perpetually packed hummus haven serves what many consider
to be the best hummus around. Beer and wine available.
Serving lunch, dinner and late-night daily.

New York magazine: Critics' Pick
Zagat: 23 food rating (very good to excellent)
Time Out New York: Critics' Pick
The Village Voice: Critics' Pick

NEW YORK CITY
⭐**TOP100** Il Cortile
125 Mulberry St (bet Canal and Hester Sts)
New York, NY 10013
(212) 226-6060

Neighborhood Map: **Little Italy/NoLita**
Category: **Italian**
Price Range: **$$$**
www.ilcortile.com

Among the tourist-swarmed whirlwind of gelaterias, maitre d's hassling passersby to eat in their restaurants, and plastic-patio-furniture laden sidewalks, Il Cortile is a ray of light for refinement and real Italian cuisine on Mulberry Street. With more than 30 years of experience, this Little Italy staple attracts the business elite, couples out for a romantic evening, and those in the know who don't waste their time looking at every menu displayed on the street. The bright dining room is decorated with foliage and Roman sculptures, and a tall glass ceiling encloses the famed Garden Room and lets sunlight shine through. Chef Michael DeGeorgio's vast menu consists of large portions of rustic Italian classics. Appetizers such as the seafood salad or the sausage, artichoke and mozzarella pie start the meal. Entrées include veal scaloppini, halibut wrapped with bacon, and gnocchi stuffed with chicken, spinach and mascarpone cheese. The patio out front and the airy cocktail lounge are popular spots as well. Full bar. Serving lunch, dinner and late-night daily.

Zagat: 23 food rating (very good to excellent)

NEW YORK CITY ★TOP100 Il Mulino

86 W 3rd St (bet Sullivan and Thompson Sts)
New York, NY 10012
(212) 673-3783

Neighborhood Map: **Greenwich Village**
Category: **Italian**
Price Range: **$$$$**
www.ilmulino.com

Opened by brothers Fernando and Gino Masci in 1981, this somewhat-cramped Greenwich Village classic has remained much the same since its founding. The dining room is Old World (though sparse), as is the doting, tuxedo-clad service. The prices, well … not so much. But you'll find heaping portions of classic fine-dining Italian fare infused with enough garlic to keep any army of vampires, or just your date, far away from your bedroom at night. Jumbo shrimp scampi, sausage pappardelle, chicken Parmesan, and veal osso buco in a red wine sauce with porcini mushrooms headline the menu, but regulars will instruct you to pay attention to the laundry list of specials from your polished server. Securing reservations proves to be a trying task, as the phone is rarely answered.

But they are nonetheless required. Full bar with extensive wine list. Serving lunch Mon–Fri, dinner Mon–Sat. Closed Sun.

New York magazine: Critics' Pick
Zagat: 27 food rating (extraordinary to perfection)

'Inoteca

★ **BEST WINE BAR ON THE LOWER EAST SIDE**
98 Rivington St (near Ludlow St)
New York, NY 10002
(212) 614-0473

Neighborhood Map: **Lower East Side**
Categories: **Brunch, Italian, Wine Bar**
Price Range: **$$**
www.inotecanyc.com

A perfect spot to nosh with friends and share some wine, a plate of cheeses, some salume and a panini or three. Beer and wine available. Serving lunch, dinner and late-night daily. Sat–Sun brunch 10 am–4 pm.

New York magazine: ★ (good); Critics' Pick
Zagat: 23 food rating (very good to excellent)
Time Out New York: Critics' Pick
The Village Voice: Critics' Pick

Insieme

★ **BEST HOTEL RESTAURANT IN MIDTOWN WEST/ THEATER DISTRICT**
777 7th Ave (near 51st St, The Michelangelo)
New York, NY 10019
(212) 582-1310

Neighborhood Map: **Midtown West/Theater District**
Categories: **Breakfast, Contemporary, Hotel Restaurant, Italian**
Price Range: **$$$**
www.restaurantinsieme.com

Diners can choose between traditional Italian dishes or more contemporary Italian creations. Either way, the quality and taste are consistently excellent. Reservations suggested. Full bar. Serving breakfast daily, lunch Mon–Fri, dinner Mon–Sat.

Michelin Guide: ★ (a very good restaurant in its category)
The New York Times: ★★ (very good)
New York magazine: ★★ (very good); Critics' Pick
Zagat: 24 food rating (very good to excellent)

Island Burgers & Shakes

766 9th Ave (bet 51st and 52nd Sts)
New York, NY 10019
(212) 307-7934

Neighborhood Map: **Midtown West/Theater District**
Category: **Burgers**
Price Range: **$**
http://island.ypguides.net

Over a dozen creative burgers and just as many chicken
churascos make this "Hell's Kitchen beach town burger joint"
a great choice for some cheap eats. No fries are served, but
the delicious shakes make a fine substitute. Beer and wine
available. Serving lunch and dinner daily.

New York magazine: Critics' Pick
Zagat: 22 food rating (very good to excellent)

123

Ithaka

★ **BEST GREEK ON THE UPPER EAST SIDE**
308 E 86th St (near 2nd Ave)
New York, NY 10028
(212) 628-9100

Neighborhood Map: **Upper East Side**
Category: **Greek**
Price Range: **$$**
www.ithakarestaurant.com

A romantic taverna-like space that's home to consistently
superb classic Greek dishes. Full bar. Serving lunch Sat–Sun,
dinner nightly.

Zagat: 21 food rating (very good to excellent)

Jane

★ **BEST AMERICAN TRADITIONAL IN GREENWICH VILLAGE**

100 W Houston St (bet LaGuardia and Thompson Sts)
New York, NY 10012
(212) 254-7000

Neighborhood Map: **Greenwich Village**
Categories: **American Traditional, Brunch**
Price Range: **$$**
www.ctrnyc.com/JANE/index.html

A reliable neighborhood American restaurant, Jane is particularly packed on weekends for its famed brunch boasting the likes of lobster eggs Benedict, vanilla bean French toast and the self-claimed "Best Bloody Mary." Full bar. Serving lunch and dinner daily, late-night Fri–Sat. Sat–Sun brunch.

The New York Times: Top Pick
Zagat: 21 food rating (very good to excellent)
Time Out New York: Critics' Pick

124

NEW YORK CITY ★TOP100 Jean Georges

1 Central Park W (bet 60th and 61st Sts, at Trump International Hotel & Tower)
New York, NY 10023
(212) 299-3900

Neighborhood Map: **Upper West Side**
Category: **French**
Price Range: **$$$$$**
www.jean-georges.com

While the setting inside the Trump International Hotel & Tower and the correspondingly stiff prices certainly would suggest that Jean Georges is the ultimate memory-making venue, writer Hal Rubenstein, for one, once advised in *New York* magazine forgoing anniversaries and marriage proposals here. That's because no wannabe groom wants his multi-carat offering to be outshined by the seven-course dinner tasting at this restaurant with a Mobil Five-Star rating. Run by world-famous chef Jean-Georges Vongerichten, the dining room's floor-to-ceiling windows offer beautiful views of the city that can be enjoyed from romantic tableside settees. The menu, and that of the more casual and accessible (read less expensive) Nougatine restaurant inside Jean Georges, blends French, American and Indochinese ingredients. The three-course, prix fixe dinner menu offers a virtual bonanza of bewitching combinations, including sea scallops with caramelized cauliflower and caper-raisin emulsion; young garlic soup with thyme and sautéed frog legs; and arctic char, asparagus and oyster. Full bar. Serving lunch and dinner Mon–Fri. Closed Sun.

Michelin Guide: ★★★ (exceptional cuisine and worth the journey)
The New York Times: ★★★★ (extraordinary); Top Pick
New York magazine: ★★★★ (exceptional; consistently elite); Critics' Pick
Zagat: 28 food rating (extraordinary to perfection)
Time Out New York: Critics' pick

Joe's Pizza

Neighborhood Map: **Brooklyn (Midwood)**
1621 Kings Hwy (near E 16th St)
Brooklyn, NY 11229
(718) 339-4525

Neighborhood Map: **Greenwich Village**
7 Carmine St (near Bleecker St)
New York, NY 10014
(212) 366-1182

Category: **Pizza**
Price Range: **$**
www.joespizza.com

This no-frills Greenwich Village classic is home to some of the most celebrated thin-crust slices in New York. Also with a location in Brooklyn, Joe's astounds the crowds with plain slices and fresh mozzarella and Sicilian pies. Keep an eye out for Joe's next time *Spider-Man 2* is on the tube: Your friendly neighborhood Spider-Man works as a delivery boy there under his alias, Peter Parker. No alcohol available. Serving lunch, dinner and late-night daily.

New York magazine: ★★★ (generally excellent); Critics' Pick
Zagat: 23 food rating (very good to excellent)
Time Out New York: Critics' Pick

Joe's Shanghai

Neighborhood Map: **Chinatown**
9 Pell St (bet Bowery and Mott Sts)
New York, NY 10013
(212) 233-8888

★ BEST CHINESE IN MIDTOWN WEST/THEATER DISTRICT
Neighborhood Map: **Midtown West/Theater District**
24 W 56th St (near 5th Ave)
New York, NY 10019
(212) 333-3868

Categories: **Chinese, Dumplings, Seafood**
Price Range: **$$**
www.joeshanghairestaurants.com

Best known for their soup dumplings — as in the soup is
inside the dumplings — served in hot bamboo steamers,
Joe's has an extensive menu that numbers 149 different
dishes. Beer available. BYOB. Cash only. Serving lunch and
dinner Mon–Sat. Closed Sun.

The New York Times: ★★ (very good); Top Pick
Zagat: 22 food rating (very good to excellent)

126

JoJo

160 E 64th St (bet Lexington and 3rd Aves)
New York, NY 10021
(212) 223-5656

Neighborhood Map: **Upper East Side**
Categories: **Brunch, French**
Price Range: **$$$**
www.jean-georges.com

This warm and elegant bistro is a member of the Jean-Georges
family of restaurants. Reservations suggested. Full bar. Serving
lunch and dinner daily. Sat–Sun brunch noon–3:30pm.

Michelin Guide: ★ (a very good restaurant in its category)
The New York Times: ★★★ (excellent); Top Pick
New York magazine: ★★ (very good); Critics' Pick
Zagat: 24 food rating (very good to excellent)
Time Out New York: Critics' Pick

Jumbo Hot Dogs

★ BEST HOT DOGS IN CHINATOWN

149 Canal St (near Bowery St)
New York, NY 10002
(212) 925-8827

Neighborhood Map: **Chinatown**
Category: **Hot Dogs**
Price Range: **$**

They're great, and they're only a dollar. Seriously. No alcohol available. Serving lunch and dinner daily.

The Village Voice: Critics' Pick

Katz's Delicatessen

205 E Houston St (near Ludlow St)
New York, NY 10002
(212) 254-2246

Neighborhood Map: **Lower East Side**
Categories: **Breakfast, Brunch, Deli**
Price Range: **$$**
www.katzdeli.com

Calling Katz's a New York institution would be an understatement. This famous deli, which opened in 1888, doles out some of the world's most delicious knishes, hot dogs, and corned beef and pastrami sandwiches. Beer available. Serving breakfast, lunch and dinner daily, late-night Fri–Sat.

The New York Times: ★ (good); Top Pick
New York magazine: Critics' Pick
Zagat: 23 food rating (very good to excellent)
Time Out New York: Critics' Pick
The Village Voice: Critics' Pick

127

Keens Steakhouse

72 W 36th St (near 6th Ave)
New York, NY 10018
(212) 947-3636

Neighborhood Map: **Garment District**

Category: **Steak House**
Price Range: **$$$$**
www.keens.com

Legendary mutton chops and superior cuts of dry-aged steaks, as well as a great pub menu, have been drawing locals to Keens since 1885. Reservations suggested. Full bar. Serving lunch Mon–Fri, dinner nightly.

The New York Times: ★★ (very good); Top Pick
New York magazine: Critics' Pick
Zagat: 24 food rating (very good to excellent)
Time Out New York: Critics' Pick

Ki Sushi

122 Smith St (bet Dean and Pacific Sts)
Brooklyn, NY 11201
(718) 935-0575

Neighborhood Map: **Brooklyn (Boerum Hill)**
Category: **Japanese/Sushi**
Price Range: **$$**

Beautiful sushi is served in a beautiful setting, and it's not a bad deal, either. Beer, wine and sake available. Serving lunch and dinner daily, late-night Fri–Sat.

Zagat: 26 food rating (extraordinary to perfection)

The Kitchen Club

★ **BEST ASIAN FUSION IN LITTLE ITALY/NOLITA**
30 Prince St (near Mott St)
New York, NY 10012
(212) 274-0025

Neighborhood Map: **Little Italy/NoLita**
Categories: **Asian Fusion, Contemporary, Dumplings**
Price Range: **$$$**
www.thekitchenclub.com

Run by Dutch chef/owner Marja Samsom and her omni-present French bulldog (an integral part of the restaurant), The Kitchen Club delights with some of the best dumplings in town and quirky contemporary cuisine with heavy-handed

Japanese influence. Reservations suggested. Beer, wine and sake available. Serving lunch and dinner daily.

Zagat: 21 food rating (very good to excellent)

Kittichai

60 Thompson St (near Broome St, 60 Thompson hotel)
New York, NY 10012
(212) 219-2000

Neighborhood Map: **SoHo**
Categories: **Breakfast, Brunch, Hotel Restaurant, Thai**
Price Range: **$$$**
www.kittichairestaurant.com

Modern and enticing Thai dishes from chef Ian Chalermkittichai are served in the sleek and stylish SoHo digs of the boutique 60 Thompson hotel. Full bar. Serving breakfast, lunch and dinner daily, late-night Thu–Sat. Sat–Sun brunch 11 am–2:45 pm.

The New York Times: ★★ (very good); Top Pick
New York magazine: ★★ (very good); Critics' Pick
Zagat: 22 food rating (very good to excellent)
Time Out New York: Critics' Pick

Kuma Inn

★ **BEST ASIAN FUSION ON THE LOWER EAST SIDE**
113 Ludlow St, 2nd Fl (near Delancey St)
New York, NY 10002
(212) 353-8866

Neighborhood Map: **Lower East Side**
Categories: **Asian Fusion, Small Plates**
Price Range: **$$**
www.kumainn.com

Mouth-watering flavors and spices abound at this neighborhood favorite turning out tapas-style Asian dishes. No alcohol available. BYOB. Cash only. Serving dinner Tue–Sun, late-night Fri–Sat. Closed Mon.

The New York Times: Top Pick
New York magazine: Critics' Pick
Zagat: 24 food rating (very good to excellent)

Time Out New York: Critics' Pick
The Village Voice: Critics' Pick

L'Atelier de Joël Robuchon

★ **BEST HOTEL RESTAURANT IN MIDTOWN EAST/**
   MURRAY HILL

57 E 57th St (near Park Ave, Four Seasons Hotel)
New York, NY 10022
(212) 350-6658

Neighborhood Map: **Midtown East/Murray Hill**
Categories: **Contemporary, French, Hotel Restaurant,**
   Small Plates
Price Range: **$$$$**
www.fourseasons.com/newyorkfs/dining.html

Part of a global franchise, this high-end French restaurant
in the Four Seasons Hotel is best known for its
contemporary small plates and for the bar seating with a
full view into the kitchen. Reservations suggested. Full bar.
Serving dinner nightly.

Michelin Guide: ★ (a very good restaurant in its category)
The New York Times: ★★★ (excellent); Top Pick
New York magazine: ★★★ (generally excellent); Critics' Pick
Zagat: 28 food rating (extraordinary to perfection)

L'Ecole

462 Broadway (near Grand St)
New York, NY 10013
(212) 219-3300

Neighborhood Map: **SoHo**
Category: **French**
Price Range: **$$$$**
www.frenchculinary.com/lecole.htm

The restaurant of The French Culinary Institute on Broadway,
L'Ecole is a true study in French cuisine, as dishes are prepared
each day by students. The $42 prix fixe dinner is quite a steal.
Full bar. Serving lunch Mon–Fri, dinner Mon–Sat. Closed Sun.

Zagat: 25 food rating (very good to excellent)

L'Express

★ BEST BISTRO IN UNION SQUARE/FLATIRON

249 Park Ave S (bet 19th and 20th Sts)
New York, NY 10003
(212) 254-5858

Neighborhood Map: **Union Square/Flatiron**
Categories: **Bistro, Breakfast, Brunch, French**
Price Range: **$$**
www.lexpressnyc.com

Inspired by France's second city, Lyon, L'Express is almost all things to all diners and is open 24/7. From basic breakfasts to steak frites, pig's feet and braised tripe, something on the menu will pique your interest at any time of day. Full bar. Open 24 hours. Sat–Sun brunch 10 am–5 pm.

The New York Times: Top Pick
Zagat: 17 food rating (good to very good)

La Bergamote

★ BEST CAFÉ IN CHELSEA

Neighborhood Map: **Chelsea**
169 9th Ave (near 20th St)
New York, NY 10011
(212) 627-9010

★ BEST CAFÉ IN MIDTOWN WEST/THEATER DISTRICT

Neighborhood Map: **Midtown West/Theater District**
515 W 52nd St (bet 10th and 11th Aves)
New York, NY 10019
(212) 586-2429

Categories: **Bakery, Breakfast, Café, Dessert, French**
Price Range: **$**

One small taste of a pastry at this tiny, quintessentially French shop will leave you tearfully belting "La Marseillaise." Before you get carried away with dessert (and singing), be sure to try one of the baguette sandwiches from the display case. No alchohol available. Serving during breakfast, lunch and early dinner hours daily.

Zagat: 24 food rating (very good to excellent)

131

La Esquina

★ **BEST MEXICAN IN LITTLE ITALY/NOLITA**

106 Kenmare St (bet Cleveland Pl and Lafayette St)
New York, NY 10012
(646) 613-7100

Neighborhood Map: **Little Italy/NoLita**
Categories: **Breakfast, Brunch, Mexican**
Price Range: **Taqueria $ Brasserie $$**
www.esquinanyc.com

Locals flock to this fun setting for great Mexican food,
including fabulous grilled corn. Full bar. Serving breakfast,
lunch, dinner and late-night daily.

The New York Times: ★ (good)
Zagat: 22 food rating (very good to excellent)

La Fonda Boricua

★ **BEST PUERTO RICAN IN HARLEM**

169 E 106th St (bet Lexington and 3rd Aves)
New York, NY 10029
(212) 410-7292

Neighborhood Map: **Harlem**
Categories: **Latin/South American, Puerto Rican**
Price Range: **$$**
www.fondaboricua.com

This restaurant in Spanish Harlem is a community gathering
spot for all things Puerto Rico. You'll find lively environs
characterized by exposed brick walls covered in paintings,
but no printed menus here. Try the *arroz con pollo*. Full bar.
Serving lunch and dinner daily.

The New York Times: Top Pick

NEW YORK CITY
★TOP100 La Gioconda

226 E 53rd St (bet 2nd and 3rd Aves)
New York, NY 10022
(212) 371-3536

Neighborhood Map: **Midtown East/Murray Hill**

Category: **Italian**
Price Range: **$$**
www.lagiocondany.com

This Midtown gem, which bears the Italian name of da Vinci's *Mona Lisa*, is twice as interesting and enigmatic as any Dan Brown novel. The lady herself adorns an exposed brick wall, and her eyes seem to follow the tasty Tuscan pastas as they pass through the tiny dining room, which, though unremarkable, has a distinctly cozy neighborhood feel. Begin with grilled calamari over julienned zucchini or a Caprese with plum tomatoes, house-made mozzarella and roasted peppers. The next course brings pastas such as pappardelle with lamb ragout and *tagliolini* with porcini mushrooms, prosciutto, tomato and smoked mozzarella. Grilled lamb chops, veal saltimbocca and a couple of fish preparations round out the menu. Reflecting on your meal, you may just conclude that the Renaissance masters owed much of their inspiration to delicious northern Italian cuisine. Reservations suggested. Beer and wine available. Serving lunch Mon–Fri, dinner nightly.

Zagat: 20 food rating (very good to excellent)

La Grenouille

★ **BEST FRENCH IN MIDTOWN EAST/MURRAY HILL**
3 E 52nd St (near 5th Ave)
New York, NY 10022
(212) 752-1495

Neighborhood Map: **Midtown East/Murray Hill**
Category: **French**
Price Range: **$$$$**
www.la-grenouille.com

The elegant dining rooms and exquisite fresh flower bouquets complement the classic French menu that features seasonal ingredients and offers both à la carte and three-course prix fixe options. Jacket required. Reservations suggested. Full bar. Serving lunch and dinner Tue–Sat. Closed Sun–Mon.

The New York Times: ★★★ (excellent)
New York magazine: Critics' Pick
Zagat: 27 food rating (extraordinary to perfection)
Time Out New York: Critics' Pick

La Villa Pizzeria

Neighborhood Map: **Brooklyn (Mill Basin)**
6610 Ave U (bet 66th and 67th Sts)
Brooklyn, NY 11234
(718) 251-8030

Neighborhood Map: **Brooklyn (Park Slope)**
261 5th Ave (bet Garfield Pl and 1st St)
Brooklyn, NY 11215
(718) 499-9888

Categories: **Italian, Pizza**
Price Range: **$$**
www.lavillaparkslope.com

Real Neapolitan, thin-crust pizzas (and much more) all from
the wood-fired oven. Beer and wine available. Serving lunch
and dinner daily.

Zagat: 21 food rating (very good to excellent)
The Village Voice: Critics' Pick

134

Land Thai Kitchen/Land Northeast Thai

★ **BEST THAI ON THE UPPER WEST SIDE**
Neighborhood Map: **Upper West Side**
450 Amsterdam Ave (bet 81st and 82nd Sts)
New York, NY 10024
(212) 501-8121

★ **BEST THAI ON THE UPPER EAST SIDE**
Neighborhood Map: **Upper East Side**
1565 2nd Ave (bet 81st and 82nd Sts)
New York, NY 10028
(212) 439-1847

Category: **Thai**
Price Range: **$$**
www.landthaikitchen.com

Chef/owner David Bank, a Bangkok native, displays panache
with sweet and spicy Thai flavors at these small, sleek Uptown
eateries. Full bar. Serving lunch and dinner daily.

The New York Times: Top Pick
Zagat: 22 food rating (very good to excellent)

Landmarc
Neighborhood Map: **Midtown West/Theater District**
10 Columbus Cir, 3rd Fl (near 60th St, Time Warner Center)
New York, NY 10019
(212) 823-6123

★ BEST BISTRO IN TRIBECA
Neighborhood Map: **TriBeCa**
179 W Broadway (bet Leonard and Worth Sts)
New York, NY 10013
(212) 343-3883

Categories: **Bistro, Brunch, Contemporary, French, Italian**
Price Range: **$$$**
www.landmarc-restaurant.com

A contemporary French bistro with Italian influences —
"French-and-Italian comfort food," as *Time Out New York*
characterizes it — featuring modest markups on an extensive
wine list of both full and half bottles. Full bar. Serving lunch
Mon–Fri, dinner and late-night nightly. Sat–Sun brunch.

The New York Times: ★ (good); Top Pick
New York magazine: ★ (good); Critics' Pick
Zagat: 20 food rating (very good to excellent)
Time Out New York: Critics' Pick
The Village Voice: Critics' Pick

135

NEW YORK CITY
★TOP100 Lazzara's Pizza Cafe

★ BEST PIZZA IN THE GARMENT DISTRICT
Neighborhood Map: **Garment District**
221 W 38th St (upstairs, bet 7th and 8th Aves)
New York, NY 10018
(212) 944-7792

★ BEST PIZZA IN MIDTOWN WEST/THEATER DISTRICT
Neighborhood Map: **Midtown West/Theater District**
617 9th Ave (bet 43rd and 44th Sts)

New York, NY 10036
(212) 245-4440

Categories: **Italian, Pizza**
Price Range: **$$**
www.lazzaraspizza.com

Though no three people will agree on what can make a pizza dynamic — crust consistency, cheese, how the toppings work together, how the toppings work independently, source of heating, foldable or knife-and-forkable, and so on — Lazzara's definitely turns out some of the most unique pies in town. The square, Sicilian pies have a thin, chewy crust. And those who contend that it's sauce that makes (or breaks) pizza are in for a treat, as this tomato sauce comes with quite a kick and a touch of basil. Founded in 1985 by brothers Sebastian and Tony Lazzara, this small second-story café in the Garment District sports a casually elegant look, with exposed brick, high ceilings, white tablecloths and mirrors. Lunch hours can be busy, and the dining room is narrow, so you may end up elbow to elbow with your neighbor at one of the long tables. Pizza comes in whole pies, half pies and even by the slice (refreshing for a sit-down pizza place), and the toppings list is extensive, with everything from sun-dried tomatoes and salami to sautéed broccoli, clams and shrimp. A number of heros, pastas and dinner entrées round out the menu. A second location recently popped up in Hell's Kitchen. Beer and wine available. Serving lunch Mon–Fri, dinner Tue–Fri. Closed Sat–Sun.

New York magazine: Critics' Pick

NEW YORK CITY **TOP100** Le Bernardin

★ **BEST SEAFOOD IN NYC**
155 W 51st St (bet 6th and 7th Aves)
New York, NY 10019
(212) 554-1515

Neighborhood Map: **Midtown West/Theater District**
Categories: **French, Seafood**
Price Range: **$$$$$**
www.le-bernardin.com

The only restaurant to maintain all four of *The New York*

136

Times' stars for its two-decade lifespan, Le Bernardin was born from the dreams of French-born/Michelin-starred/brother-sister duo Maguy and Gilbert Le Coze. *Gourmet* magazine's once-No. 10 pick on its America's Top 50 Restaurants list came from Parisian beginnings to Manhattan's Equitable Building (between 6th and 7th) in 1986. The principles of purity acquired in the Le Coze's small Brittany fishing village haven't faltered since, even after Gilbert's unexpected death brought Eric Ripert to the team. The conscientious Ripert consistently shuns a celebrity-chef media circuit in favor of Le Bernardin's kitchen, from which his impeccably prepared French seafood dishes with Asian accents — from sea urchin risotto to wild striped bass in bouillabaisse — continually win over the food world's toughest critics with depth and subtlety of flavor. Jacket required. Reservations required. Full bar. Serving lunch Mon–Fri, dinner Mon–Sat. Closed Sun.

Michelin Guide: ★★★ (exceptional cuisine and worth the journey)
The New York Times: ★★★★ (extraordinary); Top Pick
New York magazine: ★★★★★ (ethereal; almost perfect); Critics' Pick
Zagat: 28 food rating (extraordinary to perfection)

137

Les Halles

★ BEST BRASSERIE IN GRAMERCY/MADISON PARK
Neighborhood Map: **Gramercy/Madison Park**
411 Park Ave S (near 29th St)
New York, NY 10016
(212) 679-4111

★ BEST BRASSERIE IN THE FINANCIAL DISTRICT
Neighborhood Map: **Financial District**
15 John St (near Broadway)
New York, NY 10038
(212) 285-8585

Categories: **Brasserie, Breakfast, Brunch, French**
Price Range: **$$**
www.leshalles.net

Chef/author/TV persona Anthony Bourdain will eat anything once. Thankfully, you can dine more selectively (no live cobras or fermented shark on the menu) at his casual brasseries in

Gramercy Park and the Financial District. With more than five variations of steak frites and a butcher shop in the front of the house, a taste of Paris has never sounded so sweet to meat mongers. Full bar. Serving breakfast, lunch, dinner and late-night daily. Sat–Sun brunch.

The New York Times: Top Pick
Zagat: 19 food rating (good to very good)
Time Out New York: Critics' Pick

The Little Owl

★ **BEST BRUNCH IN THE WEST VILLAGE/MEATPACKING DISTRICT**

90 Bedford St (near Grove St)
New York, NY 10014
(212) 741-4695

Neighborhood Map: **West Village/Meatpacking District**
Categories: **Brunch, Contemporary**
Price Range: **$$$**
www.thelittleowlnyc.com

Friendly service and an exceptionally comfortable and cozy atmosphere make this corner favorite a go-to spot for brunch. (Fontina sausage buns beneath poached eggs, greens and hollandaise make for a truly sensational breakfast experience.) But dinner should definitely not be overlooked. Beer and wine available. Serving lunch Tue–Sun, dinner nightly. Sat–Sun brunch.

The New York Times: ★★ (very good); Top Pick
New York magazine: ★★ (very good); Critics' Pick
Zagat: 25 food rating (very good to excellent)
The Village Voice: Critics' Pick

Locanda Vini & Olii

129 Gates Ave (bet Cambridge Pl and Grand Ave)
Brooklyn, NY 11238
(718) 622-9202

Neighborhood Map: **Brooklyn (Clinton Hill)**
Category: **Italian**
Price Range: **$$$**
www.locandany.com

The daily changing and heavily Tuscan menu at this Clinton Hill trattoria is anything but predictable. At this converted pharmacy, a bottle of wine or a selection from the dessert cart will cure what ails you. Reservations suggested. Beer and wine available. Serving dinner Tue–Sun. Closed Mon.

New York magazine: Critics' Pick
Zagat: 25 food rating (very good to excellent)

Lovely Day

★ **BEST THAI IN LITTLE ITALY/NOLITA**
196 Elizabeth St (near Prince St)
New York, NY 10012
(212) 925-3310

Neighborhood Map: **Little Italy/NoLita**
Categories: **Brunch, Thai**
Price Range: **$**

This enigmatic little café in NoLita serves Thai noodles and curries amid red boothed, diner-esque environs. Unorthodox brunch specialties and colorful cocktails shine. Full bar. Serving lunch and dinner daily. Sat–Sun brunch 11 am–5 pm.

Time Out New York: Critics' Pick

Lucali

575 Henry St (near 1st Pl)
Brooklyn, NY 11231
(718) 858-4086

Neighborhood Map: **Brooklyn (Carroll Gardens)**
Category: **Pizza**
Price Range: **$$**

Smoke from the wood-fired ovens fills the air at this Carroll Gardens sit-down pizza place that oozes homeyness and neighborhood charm. And the crispy, thin-crust pizzas made by chefs right there in the open dining room are sure to please all tastes. No alcohol available. BYOB. Cash only. Serving dinner Wed–Mon. Closed Tue.

The New York Times: Top Pick
New York magazine: Critics' Pick

Zagat: 27 food rating (extraordinary to perfection)

Lucky Strike

59 Grand St (bet W Broadway and Wooster St)
New York, NY 10013
(212) 941-0772

Neighborhood Map: **SoHo**
Categories: **American Traditional, Bistro, Brunch**
Price Range: **$$**
www.luckystrikeny.com

Though perhaps not known for culinary perfection, Lucky
Strike is a comfortable neighborhood bistro with solid
standards. Even better, it's open late. Nothing like a bar
steak with roquefort butter and fries at 2 in the morning. Full
bar. Serving lunch Mon–Fri, dinner and late-night nightly.
Sat–Sun brunch noon–4:30 pm.

New York magazine: Critics' Pick
Zagat: 16 food rating (good to very good)

140

NEW YORK CITY ★TOP100 Lupa

170 Thompson St (bet Bleecker and Houston Sts)
New York, NY 10012
(212) 982-5089

Neighborhood Map: **Greenwich Village**
Category: **Italian**
Price Range: **$$**
www.luparestaurant.com

Much like the she-wolf (for which the restaurant is named)
that nursed budding city planners Romulus and Remus to
health, Lupa has nourished Greenwich Village with some of
the city's best and most accessible Italian fare since opening
in 1999. Owned by a veritable who's who among restaurateurs
(Mario Batali, Joseph Bastianich, Jason Denton and chef/
partner Mark Ladner), Lupa overlooks busy, student-filled
Thompson Street through an open storefront decorated with
spruce trees. The front dining room is just as busy, with a
convivial, slightly noisy atmosphere given the proximity of the
bar area and the closeness of tables. A brick archway leads to

the more spacious back dining room. Cured meats and small seafood bites such as melt-in-your mouth house-made speck or the sardines with cracked wheat lead the menu while primi consist of soft ricotta gnocchi and the slightly spicy *bucatini all' amatriciana*. Main courses include skate with clams and rabe, or the succulent, fall-apart (no knife needed) pork shoulder. Reservations suggested. Full bar. Serving lunch, dinner and late-night daily.

The New York Times: Top Pick
New York magazine: ★★ (very good); Critics' Pick
Zagat: 25 food rating (very good to excellent)
Time Out New York: Critics' Pick

Lure Fishbar

142 Mercer St (near Prince St)
New York, NY 10012
(212) 431-7676

Neighborhood Map: **SoHo**
Categories: **Brunch, Japanese/Sushi, Oysters, Seafood**
Price Range: **$$$**
www.lurefishbar.com

141

An excellent raw bar, fresh sushi choices and other seafood specialties make this SoHo spot a standout. Full bar. Serving lunch Mon–Fri, dinner nightly, late-night Fri–Sat. Sat–Sun brunch 11:30 am–3:30 pm.

The New York Times: ★ (good)
New York magazine: Critics' Pick
Zagat: 23 food rating (very good to excellent)
Time Out New York: Critics' Pick

Luz

★ BEST LATIN/SOUTH AMERICAN IN BROOKLYN
177 Vanderbilt Ave (bet Myrtle and Willoughby Aves)
Brooklyn, NY 11205
(718) 246-4000

Neighborhood Map: **Brooklyn (Fort Greene)**
Categories: **Brunch, Latin/South American**
Price Range: **$$**
www.luzrestaurant.com

Contemporary Latin American flair without an ounce of cheesiness makes this Fort Greene spot a great place to sample some Nuevo Latino favorites. The house-made guava marmalade is unique and delicious, and don't leave without trying the simple rice and beans. Reservations suggested. Full bar. Serving lunch Mon–Fri, dinner nightly, late-night Thu–Sat. Sun brunch 11 am–3:30 pm.

New York magazine: Critics' Pick
Zagat: 24 food rating (very good to excellent)

Malatesta Trattoria
649 Washington St (near Christopher St)
New York, NY 10014
(212) 741-1207

Neighborhood Map: **West Village/Meatpacking District**
Categories: **Brunch, Italian**
Price Range: **$$**

Here, the West Village meets pretty much any family-owned trattoria across Italy, as this endearing neighborhood dining room strikes all the notes of the mother country: hearty, affordable food in a space that lends itself to tarrying. Beer and wine available. Cash only. Serving dinner nightly. Sat–Sun brunch noon–4 pm.

Zagat: 23 food rating (very good to excellent)
The Village Voice: Critics' Pick

Mamoun's
Neighborhood Map: **East Village/NoHo**
22 St. Marks Pl (bet 2nd and 3rd Aves)
New York, NY 10003
(212) 387-7747

★ BEST MIDDLE EASTERN IN GREENWICH VILLAGE
Neighborhood Map: **Greenwich Village**
119 Macdougal St (near W 3rd St)
New York, NY 10012
(212) 674-8685

Category: **Middle Eastern**
Price Range: **$**

142

www.mamounsfalafel.com

Falafel lovers simply cannot get enough of this hole-in-the-wall Middle Eastern eatery. With absolutely no room to sit down inside, locals line the street, hungrily downing these tasty (and messy) sandwiches. No alcohol available. Cash only. Serving lunch, dinner and late-night daily.

The Village Voice: Critics' Pick

MarkJoseph Steakhouse

★ **BEST STEAK HOUSE IN THE FINANCIAL DISTRICT**
261 Water St (near Peck Slip)
New York, NY 10038
(212) 277-0020

Neighborhood Map: **Financial District**
Category: **Steak House**
Price Range: **$$$$**
www.markjosephsteakhouse.com

143

MarkJoseph, modeled after Peter Luger's, is a virtual beef emporium, the kind of place where a cowboy might go if he ever found himself in Manhattan. He'd want to put on his best britches, though, as this ain't a sawdust-on-the-floor kind of place. Reservations suggested. Full bar. Serving lunch Mon–Fri, dinner Mon–Sat. Closed Sun.

The New York Times: ★ (good)
New York magazine: Critics' Pick
Zagat: 24 food rating (very good to excellent)

NEW YORK CITY **★TOP100** Mary's Fish Camp/
Brooklyn Fish Camp

★ **BEST SEAFOOD IN THE WEST VILLAGE/MEATPACKING DISTRICT**
Neighborhood Map: **West Village/Meatpacking District**
64 Charles St (near W 4th St)
New York, NY 10014
(646) 486-2185

★ **BEST SEAFOOD IN BROOKLYN**
Neighborhood Map: **Brooklyn (Park Slope)**
162 5th Ave (near Degraw St)
Brooklyn, NY 11217
(718) 783-3264

Category: **Seafood**
Price Range: **$$**
www.marysfishcamp.com

West Village campers are exempt from making pinecone
birdfeeders at Mary's Fish Camp and its Brooklyn outpost,
but they may feel like they've taken a swimming test: The
exceedingly fresh fish is full of the flavor of the ocean. Mary
Redding, formerly of Pearl Oyster Bar, moved down the street
in 2000 to found this casual, no-frills dining room. The space
conjures the feel of the Florida coast, with a beachy, airy vibe
and chalkboards announcing the temperature in Miami. But
much of the menu nods to New England, with littleneck clams,
Malpeque oysters and Maine lobster. Shellfish bouillabaisse
and seasonally changing whole fish are among other simply
prepared aquatic offerings. The main attraction that keeps
locals lining up out the door, though, are the immense, messy
lobster rolls. Beer and wine available. Serving lunch and
dinner Mon–Sat. Closed Sun.

The New York Times: Top Pick
New York magazine: ★★ (very good); Critics' Pick
Zagat: 24 food rating (very good to excellent)
Time Out New York: Critics' Pick

144

Mas

39 Downing St (near Bedford St)
New York, NY 10014
(212) 255-1790

Neighborhood Map: **Greenwich Village**
Categories: **Contemporary, French**
Price Range: **$$$**
www.masfarmhouse.com

A contemporary French farmhouse in the middle of the
city, Mas is as seasonal and savory as they come. Reservations
suggested. Full bar. Serving dinner nightly.

The New York Times: ★★ (very good); Top Pick

New York magazine: ★★ (very good); Critics' Pick
Zagat: 28 food rating (extraordinary to perfection)
Time Out New York: Critics' Pick

Masa

10 Columbus Cir, 4th Fl (near 59th St, Time Warner Center)
New York, NY 10019
(212) 823-9800

Neighborhood Map: **Midtown West/Theater District**
Category: **Japanese/Sushi**
Price Range: **$$$$$**
www.masanyc.com

There are no menus at this pricey, elite and much-hyped paean to artistic Japanese cuisine in the Time Warner Center. Instead, the chef devises meals based on seasonally available ingredients and/ or the interests and tastes of his diners. Reservations required. Full bar. Serving lunch Tue–Fri, dinner Mon–Sat. Closed Sun.

Michelin Guide: ★★★ (exceptional cuisine and worth the journey)
The New York Times: ★★★★ (extraordinary); Top Pick
New York magazine: ★★★★★ (ethereal; almost perfect); Critics' Pick
Zagat: 27 food rating (extraordinary to perfection)

145

Matsugen

241 Church St (near Leonard St)
New York, NY 10013
(212) 925-0202

Neighborhood Map: **TriBeCa**
Category: **Japanese/Sushi**
Price Range: **$$$**
www.jean-georges.com

This traditional Japanese restaurant features sushi, sashimi and Asian soba — or buckwheat noodles — in a spare dining room that includes a long communal table. Full bar. Serving dinner and late-night nightly.

The New York Times: ★★★ (excellent)
New York magazine: ★ (good); Critics' Pick

Zagat: 21 food rating (very good to excellent)
Time Out New York: Critics' Pick

Merkato 55

★ BEST AFRICAN IN THE WEST VILLAGE/MEATPACKING DISTRICT

55 Gansevoort St (near Greenwich St)
New York, NY 10014
(212) 255-8555

Neighborhood Map: **West Village/Meatpacking District**
Categories: **African, Brunch**
Price Range: **$$$**

A relative newcomer to the Meatpacking District, Merkato 55, the latest venture of renowned chef Marcus Samuelsson (of Aquavit fame), aims high with dramatic environs, upscale Pan-African cuisine and eclectic cocktails and beers to match. Save room for the coconut cake. Reservations suggested. Full bar. Serving dinner and late-night nightly. Sat–Sun brunch 11:30 am–3 pm.

The New York Times: ★ (good)
New York magazine: ★★ (very good); Critics' Pick
Zagat: 21 food rating (very good to excellent)

NEW YORK CITY ★TOP100 Mesa Grill

★ BEST SOUTHWESTERN IN NYC

102 5th Ave (bet 15th and 16th Sts)
New York, NY 10011
(212) 807-7400

Neighborhood Map: **Union Square/Flatiron**
Categories: **Brunch, Contemporary, Southwestern**
Price Range: **$$$**
www.mesagrill.com

Long before he was throwing down on the Food Network, Bobby Flay displayed his undeniable talent at the original Mesa Grill, which opened in 1991. His love for Southwestern flavors, wet and dry rubs, and grilling is still evident on the menu today. The vibrantly colored dining room is filled with a stylish happy hour crowd sipping creative margaritas and nibbling on goat cheese queso or the signature blue corn pancakes with barbecued duck. Red columns, oversized black and white photos, and kitschy Southwestern touches (multicolored plates and chairs and upholstered cactus- and cowboy-patterned booths overlooking Fifth Avenue) adorn the two-level space. Flavors are bold and the spice substantial in standout entrées such as the New Mexican spice-rubbed pork tenderloin, a chipotle-glazed rib eye and the earthy, cornmeal-crusted chile relleno with a subtly spicy and sweet red pepper sauce and balsamic vinegar. Reservations suggested. Full bar. Serving lunch Mon–Fri, dinner nightly. Sat brunch 11:30 am–2:30 pm. Sun brunch 11:30 am–3 pm.

The New York Times: ★★ (very good)
New York magazine: Critics' Pick
Zagat: 23 food rating (very good to excellent)

NEW YORK CITY
★TOP100 The Modern

9 W 53rd St (bet 5th and 6th Aves, inside the Museum of
   Modern Art)
New York, NY 10019
(212) 333-1220

147

Neighborhood Map: **Midtown West/Theater District**
Category: **Contemporary**
Price Range: **Dining Room $$$$$ Bar Room $$$**
www.themodernnyc.com

Given The Modern's home inside the Museum of Modern Art, perhaps it's fitting that even some of the restaurant's most loyal boosters grudgingly concede that chef Gabriel Kreuther's menu can be a bit pretentious. But it's arguably the best of all worlds, because for those inclined to view some entrées as "busy and a little overworked" — as an otherwise glowing *New York* magazine piece put it — there is the adjacent and more casual Bar Room, where the rustic small plates are more simple and accessible. So whereas the formal dining room's menu offers fine-herbs-braised Vermont suckling pig with parsnip pureé, roasted pineapple and natural jus scented with cardamom (!), the bar gives diners the beer-braised pork belly with sauerkraut and ginger jus. In other words, there's something to please both the fussiest foodies looking for the trendiest combinations as they overlook the MoMA's Abby Aldrich Rockefeller Sculpture Garden and the hungry walk-ins looking for fine food. Full bar. Dining Room serving lunch Mon–Fri, dinner Mon–Sat. Closed Sun. Bar Room serving lunch and dinner daily.

Michelin Guide: ★ (a very good restaurant in its category)
The New York Times: ★★ (very good); Top Pick
New York magazine: ★★★ (excellent); Critics' Pick
Zagat: 26 food rating (extraordinary to perfection)

NEW YORK CITY
★TOP100 Molyvos

871 7th Ave (bet 55th and 56th Sts)
New York, NY 10019
(212) 582-7500

Neighborhood Map: **Midtown West/Theater District**
Category: **Greek**
Price Range: **$$$**
www.molyvos.com

With a welcoming and open storefront overlooking Seventh
Avenue and lined with large planters, Molyvos has put the
chic in Greek since its 1997 opening. Warm earth tones,
long booths and ceramic urns give the dining room a homey
vibe, especially if your home happens to be on a Greek
island named Lesbos, from where owner John Livanos hails,
specifically the small village of Molyvos. From beginnings
of grilled baby octopus and flaming cheese (*saganaki*)
to the sweet finish of baklava or phyllo filled with custard
(*bougatsa*), a meal at Molyvos is a friendly, fresh and filling
experience. Entrées include classics and modern twists
alike, featuring a splendid rendition of moussaka, a simply
prepared, grilled whole fish of the day, and lamb shanks baked
in a clay pot and served with orzo, tomatoes and Kefalotyri
cheese. Affordable pre- and post-theater menus are a popular
choice for Carnegie Hall attendees. The extensive wine list
is predominantly Greek, and multiple varieties of ouzo are
available. Reservations suggested. Full bar. Serving lunch and
dinner daily. Late-night Sat.

The New York Times: ★★ (very good); Top Pick
New York magazine: Critics' Pick
Zagat: 22 food rating (very good to excellent)
Time Out New York: Critics' Pick

NEW YORK CITY
★TOP100 Momofuku Noodle Bar

★ **BEST NOODLE HOUSE IN NYC**
171 1st Ave (near 11th St)

148

New York, NY 10003
(212) 777-7773

Neighborhood Map: **East Village/NoHo**
Categories: **Asian Fusion, Japanese/Sushi, Korean,
    Noodle House**
Price Range: **$$**
www.momofuku.com

Cooking whatever the *@#$ he wants, David Chang isn't your average James Beard award-winning chef. This noodle shop cowboy has an affinity for fast food and foul language. He smokes too much. He's a French Culinary Institute grad, but he cooks some of New York's cheapest eats. When customers complained about the lack of meatless menu options, he chucked pig tails and pork belly in all but one vegetarian dish. Regardless of whatever standards he doesn't follow, chef Chang can be counted on for one thing: giant, shockingly good bowls of succulent noodles filled with Berkshire pork, braised tripe and Long Island razor clams. A move down the street to updated, enlarged digs has only added to his growing appeal, which now includes wildly popular and critically acclaimed sister restaurants Momofuku Ssäm Bar and Momofuku Ko. Beer and sake available. Serving lunch and dinner daily, late-night Fri–Sat.

The New York Times: Top Pick
New York magazine: ★ (good); Critics' Pick
Zagat: 23 food rating (very good to excellent)
The Village Voice: Critics' Pick

Momofuku Ssäm Bar

207 2nd Ave (near 13th St)
New York, NY 10003
(212) 254-3500

Neighborhood Map: **East Village/NoHo**
Categories: **Asian Fusion, Japanese/Sushi, Korean**
Price Range: **$$**
www.momofuku.com

Rockstar status still intact, David Chang opened this, his second venture, in 2006. Famous for its pork buns, Momofuku Ssäm also offers a raw bar, small plates, country ham and the extremely limited seating you'd expect. Reservations not accepted. Beer, wine and sake available. Serving lunch, dinner and late-night daily.

The New York Times: ★★ (very good); Top Pick
New York magazine: ★★★ (generally excellent); Critics' Pick
Zagat: 23 food rating (very good to excellent)

Mooncake Foods

★ BEST ASIAN FUSION IN SOHO

28 Watts St (near Thompson St)
New York, NY 10013
(212) 219-8888

Neighborhood Map: **SoHo**
Category: **Asian Fusion**
Price Range: **$**

Look no further than this family-owned SoHo spot for Pan-Asian treats (including soups, salads and sandwiches) at unbeatable prices. Beer and wine available. Cash only. Serving lunch and dinner Mon–Sat. Closed Sun.

New York magazine: Critics' Pick

NEW YORK CITY
★TOP100 Moustache

★ BEST MIDDLE EASTERN IN NYC

Neighborhood Map: **East Village/NoHo**
265 E 10th St (near 1st Ave)
New York, NY 10009
(212) 228-2022

Neighborhood Map: **West Village/Meatpacking District**
90 Bedford St (bet Barrow and Grove Sts)
New York, NY 10014
(212) 229-2220

Category: **Middle Eastern**
Price Range: **$$**

A step up from hole in the wall but obscure enough to pat yourself on the back for finding it, Moustache serves up some of the freshest jazzed-up versions of Middle Eastern classics around. The tiny, original West Village spot, with its lovely outdoor courtyard and distinctive brass tables, and one sister location (in the East Village) offer out-of-the-oven pita bread and a version of baba ghanoush that defines the dish like *Project Runway* defines style. The trademark "pitzas" are always a hit, but we recommend the excellent lentil soup or any dish with lamb. Service is not the quickest in the city, so plan accordingly. Reservations not accepted. Beer and wine available. Cash only. Serving lunch, dinner and late-night daily.

The New York Times: Top Pick
New York magazine: Critics' Pick
Zagat: 21 food rating (very good to excellent)
Time Out New York: Critics' Pick

Murray Hill Diner

222 Lexington Ave (bet 33rd and 34th Sts)
New York, NY 10016
(212) 686-6667

Neighborhood Map: **Midtown East/Murray Hill**
Categories: **Breakfast, Diner**
Price Range: **$$**

A classic New York diner devoid of any retro cuteness, Murray Hill Diner brings great breakfasts to a diverse assortment of happy customers. A variety of omelets are available, and whoever cooks the bacon clearly knows his or her way around the kitchen. Beer and wine available. Serving breakfast, lunch and dinner daily. Closes 7 pm Sun.

Murray's Bagels

★ **BEST BAGELS IN CHELSEA**
Neighborhood Map: **Chelsea**
242 8th Ave (bet 22nd and 23rd Sts)
New York, NY 10011
(646) 638-1335

★ **BEST BAGELS IN GREENWICH VILLAGE**
Neighborhood Map: **Greenwich Village**
500 Ave of the Americas (near 13th St)
New York, NY 10011
(212) 462-2830

Categories: **Bagels, Deli**

151

Price Range: **$**
www.murraysbagels.com

Don't ask for your bagel to be toasted here; they won't do it.
But do get the Everything bagel with nova cream cheese, and
see what all the fuss is about. No alcohol available. Serving
during breakfast, lunch and dinner hours daily.

New York magazine: Critics' Pick

Nam

★ BEST VIETNAMESE IN TRIBECA

110 Reade St (near W Broadway)
New York, NY 10013
(212) 267-1777

Neighborhood Map: **TriBeCa**
Category: **Vietnamese**
Price Range: **$$**
www.namnyc.com

Traditional but contemporary Vietnamese fare is served in a
nicely appointed dining room where the tables' centerpieces
are simple grass arrangements. Reservations suggested. Full
bar. Serving lunch Mon–Fri, dinner nightly.

The New York Times: Top Pick
New York magazine: Critics' Pick
Zagat: 21 food rating (very good to excellent)
Time Out New York: Critics' Pick

The Neptune Room

★ BEST SEAFOOD ON THE UPPER WEST SIDE

511 Amsterdam Ave (near 84th St)
New York, NY 10024
(212) 496-4100

Neighborhood Map: **Upper West Side**
Categories: **Brunch, Mediterranean, Oysters, Seafood**
Price Range: **$$$**
www.ctrnyc.com

The aging yacht décor seems appropriate, as this
neighborhood favorite features a full raw bar and a menu

of seafood-centric Mediterranean cuisine, not to mention a popular brunch. Full bar. Serving "sunset dinner" and dinner nightly. Sat–Sun brunch 11:30 am–2 pm.

Zagat: 21 food rating (very good to excellent)
Time Out New York: Critics' Pick

New Bo Ky

★ **BEST NOODLE HOUSE IN CHINATOWN**
80 Bayard St (near Mott St)
New York, NY 10013
(212) 406-2292

Neighborhood Map: **Chinatown**
Categories: **Chinese, Noodle House, Vietnamese**
Price Range: **$**

Decorative touches are minimal and the staff speaks little English at this Chinatown noodle shop. The extensive list of noodles and savory soups at bargain-basement prices are the main attraction here. No alcohol available. Cash only. Serving breakfast, lunch and dinner daily.

New York magazine: Critics' Pick
Zagat: 20 food rating (very good to excellent)

153

Nice Matin

201 W 79th St (near Amsterdam Ave)
New York, NY 10024
(212) 873-6423

Neighborhood Map: **Upper West Side**
Categories: **Bistro, Breakfast, Brunch, French**
Price Range: **$$**
www.nicematinnyc.com

Outdoor seating and delicious bistro fare make this a popular breakfast and brunch spot for Upper West Siders. Full bar. Serving breakfast and lunch Mon–Fri, dinner nightly. Sat–Sun brunch.

The New York Times: ★★ (very good); Top Pick
New York magazine: ★ (good); Critics' Pick
Zagat: 19 food rating (good to very good)

★TOP100 Nobu

NEW YORK CITY

105 Hudson St (near Franklin St)
New York, NY 10013
(212) 219-0500

Neighborhood Map: **TriBeCa**
Category: **Japanese/Sushi**
Price Range: **$$$**
www.noburestaurants.com

The sultan of sushi, the pharaoh of fusion, Nobu Matsuhisa
has achieved hall of fame status among restaurateurs since
opening Nobu in 1994. He's gone on to open Nobu 57 and
Nobu Next Door and has expanded his restaurant empire
internationally, but his original New York outpost in TriBeCa
remains wildly popular. The see-and-be-seen crowd as well
as those hopeful for celebrity sightings flock to this vast,
theatrical dining room, which is co-owned by Robert De Niro.
As far as sushi goes, the multi-course *omakase* is a reliable
bet. South-of-the-border influence is prevalent in ceviche
with lobster, yellowtail sashimi with jalapeño, and Nobu
sashimi tacos, but many claim that it is the cooked Japanese
fusion dishes, which Nobu popularized, that render this a
truly special dining experience. The black cod with miso is
the signature dish, while other options include halibut cheeks
with wasabi pepper sauce or squid pasta with garlic sauce.
If you can't find a seat, try Nobu Next Door, which only takes
walk-ins. Reservations suggested. Full bar. Serving lunch
Mon–Fri, dinner nightly.

The New York Times: ★★★ (excellent); Top Pick
New York magazine: ★★ (very good); Critics' Pick
Zagat: 27 food rating (extraordinary to perfection)
Time Out New York: Critics' Pick

Nobu Next Door

105 Hudson St (near Franklin St)
New York, NY 10013
(212) 334-4445

Neighborhood Map: **TriBeCa**
Category: **Japanese/Sushi**
Price Range: **$$$**
www.noburestaurants.com

154

An outgrowth of the original Japanese Nobu offering late-night dining, music and a raw bar. Full bar. Serving dinner nightly, late-night Mon–Sat.

The New York Times: ★★★ (excellent); Top Pick
New York magazine: Critics' Pick
Zagat: 27 food rating (extraordinary to perfection)
Time Out New York: Critics' Pick

Noodle Pudding

38 Henry St (bet Middagh and Cranberry Sts)
Brooklyn, NY 11201
(718) 625-3737

Neighborhood Map: **Brooklyn (Brooklyn Heights)**
Category: **Italian**
Price Range: **$$**

This off-the-beaten path cucina in Brooklyn Heights specializes in Italian comfort food — some of the best in the city, as the lines will confirm. Reservations not accepted. Full bar. Cash only. Serving dinner Tue–Sun. Closed Mon.

155

New York magazine: Critics' Pick
Zagat: 24 food rating (very good to excellent)
Time Out New York: Critics' Pick

NEW YORK CITY
★TOP100 Norma's

★ BEST BREAKFAST IN NYC
118 W 57th St (bet 6th and 7th Aves, Le Parker Meridien)
New York, NY 10019
(212) 708-7460

Neighborhood Map: **Midtown West/Theater District**
Categories: **Breakfast, Brunch, Contemporary, Hotel Restaurant**
Price Range: **$$**
www.parkermeridien.com

Forsake your faux-nutritional breakfast bar or your everyday plate of diner eggs and bacon, and start your day where breakfast is the most celebrated meal rather than an afterthought or routine. Just a few blocks south of Central

Park in the Parker Meridien, Norma's gives the first meal of the day a deluxe, over-the-top treatment. Bleary-eyed hotel guests and a young, in-the-know brunch crowd congregate in the elegant, high-ceilinged space with soft jazz in the background. A shot glass full of the fruit smoothie of the day greets every diner. Each table that orders coffee receives its own French press, so that cups may runneth over. Plates are piled high with colorful fruit and architecturally impressive pancake, crêpe and egg dishes. From the breakfast nachos (banana, pineapple and strawberry on tortilla chips, drizzled with chocolate) to foie gras brioche French toast or the $1,000 lobster frittata (with caviar), Norma's proclaims that decadence need not be reserved for 5 pm or later. The potato pancakes recipe garnered a James Beard award, as these lightly browned cakes come with a sweet, subtle carrot *payasam* and a bold, standout cranberry apple sauce. No alcohol available. Serving breakfast (all day) and lunch daily. Sat–Sun brunch 7 am–3 pm.

The New York Times: Top Pick
New York magazine: Critics' Pick
Zagat: 25 food rating (very good to excellent)
Time Out New York: Critics' Pick

Novitá

102 E 22nd St (bet Lexington Ave and Park Ave S)
New York, NY 10010
(212) 677-2222

Neighborhood Map: **Gramercy/Madison Park**
Category: **Italian**
Price Range: **$$**
www.novitanyc.com

Here you'll find updated northern Italian cuisine in a cozy Venetian atmosphere. Full bar. Serving lunch Mon–Fri, dinner nightly.

New York magazine: Critics' Pick
Zagat: 24 food rating (very good to excellent)

 **Oceana**

★ **BEST SEAFOOD IN MIDTOWN EAST/MURRAY HILL**
55 E 54th St (bet Madison and Park Aves)

New York, NY 10022
(212) 759-5941

Neighborhood Map: **Midtown East/Murray Hill**
Categories: **Contemporary, Seafood**
Price Range: **$$$$$**
www.oceanarestaurant.com

Though trend watchers are apt to think that the best years of
a restaurant opened in 1992 have set sail, in-the-know New
York foodies are still aboard the Livanos Restaurant Group's
stalwart Oceana. This Midtown home of the power lunch
offers luxury cruise ship décor with service to match, but
it's the world-class menu, well-executed and adventurous
in intention, that earns this gem its three-star *New York
Times* rating night after night. Chef Ben Pollinger explores
international waters to bring the best of the earth's oceans
to your table, pairing fresh sea bounty with unexpected
ingredients to keep the palate guessing. Sautéed soft shell
crab is dressed with cranberry beans, pancetta, hazelnuts and
saba, while crispy arctic char is offset with buckwheat spatzle
and melted leeks. The three-course tasting menus are often
the way to go, and don't miss the excellent dessert list (which
has included Concord grape "pie" and peanut butter ice
cream) and expert wine pairings. Reservations suggested. Full
bar. Serving lunch Mon–Fri, dinner Mon–Sat. Closed Sun.

Michelin Guide: ★ (a very good restaurant in its category)
The New York Times: ★★★ (excellent); Top Pick
Zagat: 26 food rating (extraordinary to perfection)
Time Out New York: Critics' Pick

Old Town Bar & Restaurant

★ BEST SPORTS BAR/PUB FOOD IN UNION SQUARE/FLATIRON

45 E 18th St (bet Broadway and Park Ave S)
New York, NY 10003
(212) 529-6732

Neighborhood Map: **Union Square/Flatiron**
Categories: **Burgers, Sports Bar/Pub Food**
Price Range: **$**
www.oldtownbar.com

Dating back to 1892, Old Town has been a watering hole
for mobsters, bootleggers (it was a speakeasy during

Prohibition), award-winning novelists (Frank McCourt, Nick Hornsby) and other such characters. These days, it's just a great place to grab a burger and a beer and take in some old New York. Full bar. Serving lunch Mon–Sat, dinner nightly.

The New York Times: Top Pick

Omai

★ BEST VIETNAMESE IN CHELSEA

158 9th Ave (bet 19th and 20th Sts)
New York, NY 10011
(212) 633-0550

Neighborhood Map: **Chelsea**
Category: **Vietnamese**
Price Range: **$$**
www.omainyc.com

Slightly difficult to find from the street, Omai proves well worth the search for upscale Vietnamese in stylish, candelit digs. Reservations suggested. Full bar. Serving dinner nightly.

New York magazine: Critics' Pick
Zagat: 23 food rating (very good to excellent)

Omen

113 Thompson St (bet Prince and Spring Sts)
New York, NY 10012
(212) 925-8923

Neighborhood Map: **SoHo**
Category: **Japanese/Sushi**
Price Range: **$$$**

Don't look for flashy presentation at the home of what *New York* magazine calls "Kyoto-style country cooking," just authentic Japanese dishes that inspire awe in adventurous eaters. Four-course prix fixe menu available. Full bar. Serving dinner and late-night nightly.

New York magazine: Critics' Pick
Zagat: 23 food rating (very good to excellent)

Oriental Garden

★ **BEST SEAFOOD IN CHINATOWN**

14 Elizabeth St (bet Bayard and Canal Sts)
New York, NY 10013
(212) 619-0085

Neighborhood Map: **Chinatown**
Categories: **Brunch, Chinese, Seafood**
Price Range: **$$**

This no-frills Chinatown dining room is full of life, what with servers buzzing around carrying dim sum delights and the tank full of aquatic edibles that will soon be on your plate. Seafood doesn't get much fresher than this. Beer, wine and sake available. Serving brunch, lunch and dinner daily.

The New York Times: ★★ (very good); Top Pick
New York magazine: ★★ (very good); Critics' Pick
Zagat: 24 food rating (very good to excellent)

The Original Chinatown Ice Cream Factory

★ **BEST ICE CREAM IN CHINATOWN**

65 Bayard St (bet Mott and Elizabeth Sts)
New York, NY 10013
(212) 608-4170

Neighborhood Map: **Chinatown**
Category: **Ice Cream**
Price Range: **$**
www.chinatownicecreamfactory.com

Celebrating more than 30 years in business, this ice cream store offers traditional as well as Asian flavors. Lychee is among the most popular. Serving during lunch and dinner hours daily.

The New York Times: Top Pick
New York magazine: Critics' Pick

 Ottimo

★ **BEST PIZZA IN UNION SQUARE/FLATIRON**

6 W 24th St (near Broadway)

New York, NY 10010
(212) 337-0074

Neighborhood Map: **Union Square/Flatiron**
Categories: **Italian, Pizza**
Price Range: **$$$**
www.ottimo-nyc.com

Naples became the birthplace of modern pizza sometime in
the late 18th century with the essential addition of tomatoes
to flatbreads — quite clever *paesanos*, eh? And while
great New York-style pizzerias and delicious grab-and-go
slices are (thankfully) a dime a dozen in the city, get back
to the roots of pizza at Ottimo, a Neapolitan restaurant (in
a Flatiron brownstone) that has garnered much acclaim
for its delicious thin-crust pies. Chef Salvatore Esposito,
a Naples native and James Beard Foundation-recognized
chef, uses exclusively imported Italian ingredients, such as
buffalo mozzarella, San Marzano tomatoes, spicy salami and
prosciutto di Parma. Neapolitan-inspired pastas and risottos
— spaghetti with clams or mussels sautéed in white wine,
or risotto with porcini mushrooms, butter, onion and pinot
grigio, for example — round out the menu and are a welcome
alternative to the oversaturation of Tuscan fare citywide. Full
bar. Serving lunch Mon–Fri, dinner Mon–Sat. Closed Sun.

160

NEW YORK CITY
★TOP100 Otto

★ **BEST PIZZA IN GREENWICH VILLAGE**

1 5th Ave (ent on 8th St)
New York, NY 10003
(212) 995-9559

Neighborhood Map: **Greenwich Village**
Categories: **Ice Cream, Italian, Pizza, Wine Bar**
Price Range: **$$**
www.ottopizzeria.com

Often the most distinguishing characteristic of pizza is how
it's cooked. And while the heated debate continues between
the coal-burning and wood-burning camps, Mario Batali has
gone outside the box with his inventive, griddle-cooked pizzas
at Otto. The red-headed super chef has put his brand on this
Greenwich Village spot with cured Italian meats and cheeses
and his trademark *lardo* (pork fat). It's a gathering spot for
students, families, scenesters and foodies alike because of its

festive atmosphere and reasonable prices, so the place stays packed and is a little chaotic at times. Eating at the bar is an attractive option for those wanting to forgo the wait. Ultra-thin-crust pizzas range from traditional to more experimental (the clams, garlic, mozzarella pizza or the potato, anchovy and ricotta pie). Gelato nearly steals the show, with Otto's famed olive oil flavor among options such as dark chocolate, pistachio and bufala ricotta. An extensive, notable wine list is composed entirely of Italian choices. Reservations suggested. Full bar. Serving lunch, dinner and late-night daily.

The New York Times: ★★ (very good); Top Pick
New York magazine: ★★ (very good); Critics' Pick
Zagat: 23 food rating (very good to excellent)
Time Out New York: Critics' Pick
The Village Voice: Critics' Pick

NEW YORK CITY
★TOP100 Ouest

2315 Broadway (near 84th St)
New York, NY 10024
(212) 580-8700

Neighborhood Map: **Upper West Side**
Categories: **Brunch, Contemporary**
Price Range: **$$$**
www.ouestny.com

While many acclaimed chefs keep their names in print by fusing odd combinations of pan-seared this and citrus-infused what-have-you, kitchen whiz Tom Valenti has earned his stellar reputation by cooking haute cuisine that people actually want to eat. His fine-dining bistro, Ouest, remains the beacon of posh on the Upper West Side, though blue blazers and khakis still fill the dining room and olives happily swim in the infamously stiff martinis in true UWS fashion. It's the menu that pushes the envelope here, and particular recommendations include roasted sturgeon and the chef's signature fall-off-the-bone braised short ribs with horseradish spatzle. Sunday brunch (11 am–2 pm) is also a treat with its jazzed-up selection of eggs any way and brioche French toast with fruit compote. Just don't miss the delectable crème fraiche panna cotta for dessert at any meal. Full bar. Serving dinner nightly. Sun brunch.

The New York Times: Top Pick

New York magazine: ★★★ (very good); Critics' Pick
Zagat: 25 food rating (very good to excellent)
Time Out New York: Critics' Pick

Pakistan Tea House

★ BEST INDIAN IN TRIBECA

176 Church St (bet Reade and Duane Sts)
New York, NY 10013
(212) 240-9800

Neighborhood Map: **TriBeCa**
Category: **Indian**
Price Range: **$**

Originally intended to cater to Muslim cab drivers, this eatery is open until 4 am and serves made-to-order tandoori breads, fish, chicken and other traditional Indian-Pakistani fare. No alcohol available. BYOB. Serving lunch, dinner and late-night daily.

The New York Times: Top Pick
The Village Voice: Critics' Pick

NEW YORK CITY
★TOP100 Pampano

209 E 49th St (bet 2nd and 3rd Aves)
New York, NY 10017
(212) 751-4545

Neighborhood Map: **Midtown East/Murray Hill**
Categories: **Contemporary, Mexican, Seafood**
Price Range: **$$$**
www.modernmexican.com/pampano

Modern Mexican cuisine continues to flourish in Manhattan, and Midtown East favorite Pampano remains one of the torchbearers for the movement. Mole and chorizo enthusiasts take note, though: Pampano specializes in Mexico's coastal cooking, meaning fresh and inventive seafood dishes. Chef/owner Richard Sandoval's (also of Maya) two-tiered dining room has airy, beachside elegance, with white walls, wicker chairs and plenty of light. Spicy guacamole and multiple varieties of ceviche (mahi mahi, tuna, halibut) headline the menu. The ocean's abundance is sizzled up and delicately sauced, from the signature lobster tacos and baby octopus

---

in a chile-serrano emulsion to whole baby red snapper and swordfish with potato-caper fondue. Reservations suggested. Full bar. Serving lunch Mon–Fri, dinner nightly.

The New York Times: ★★ (very good); Top Pick
New York magazine: ★★ (very good); Critics' Pick
Zagat: 24 food rating (very good to excellent)
Time Out New York: Critics' Pick

Paola's

245 E 84th St (bet 2nd and 3rd Aves)
New York, NY 10028
(212) 794-1890

Neighborhood Map: **Upper East Side**
Category: **Italian**
Price Range: **$$$**
www.paolasrestaurant.com

One of the lesser-known great neighborhood Italian restaurants in the city, Paola's pleases with hearty pastas (duck ravioli, veal *agnolotti*), sidewalk tables and a romantic dining room in dark red tones. Full bar. Serving dinner nightly.

163

The New York Times: ★★ (very good); Top Pick

Pastis

★ **BEST FRENCH IN THE WEST VILLAGE/MEATPACKING DISTRICT**

9 9th Ave (bet Little W 12th and W 13 Sts)
New York, NY 10014
(212) 929-4844

Neighborhood Map: **West Village/Meatpacking District**
Categories: **Bistro, Breakfast, Brunch, French**
Price Range: **$$$**
www.pastisny.com

This lively, ever-crowded Parisian-style bistro is popular with the scenesters for its late-night hours and reliably delicious bites. A notable Sunday brunch offers the likes of lobster with garlic butter and fries, a variety of egg dishes, and specialty cocktails such as a gin fizz and the French 75 (cognac, lemon juice and champagne). Reservations suggested. Full bar.

Serving breakfast and lunch Mon–Fri, dinner and late-night nightly. Sat–Sun brunch 10 am–4:30 pm.

The New York Times: ★ (good)
New York magazine: Critics' Pick
Zagat: 20 food rating (very good to excellent)

NEW YORK CITY **★TOP100** **Patsy's Pizzeria** (original)
2287 1st Ave (bet 117th and 118th Sts)
New York, NY 10035
(212) 534-9783

Neighborhood Map: **Harlem**
Categories: **Italian, Pizza**
Price Range: **$$**

Though a mini-chain bearing the same name (under different ownership, but still with better-than-average pizza) has spun off with multiple locations across Manhattan, the original Patsy's in East Harlem, which dates back to 1933, continues to be hallowed ground for pizza aficionados, including just about every construction worker who happens to be in the area around lunchtime. Sinatra is on the record claiming that these pies are "the greatest in the world. I don't care where you go, all the way to Italy, there ain't nothing like that." Quite a ringing endorsement from ol' blue eyes, but take one bite of the paper-thin-crust perfection yourself, and you may be inspired to do some crooning of your own. The undeniable secret behind the distinct charred, crispy yet slightly chewy crust has remained the same over 75 years: the coal-fired brick oven, one of the few left in the city. Throw in a tangy tomato sauce, some basil, service with a little attitude, and Rat Pack-esque décor, and you're left with a legendary slice of New York. Full bar. Cash only. Serving lunch and dinner daily, late-night Fri.

Zagat: 20 food rating (very good to excellent)

Patsy's Pizzeria
Neighborhood Map: **Chelsea**
318 W 23rd St (bet 8th and 9th Aves)
New York, NY 10011
(646) 486-7400

Neighborhood Map: **Greenwich Village**
67 University Pl (bet 10th and 11th Sts)
New York, NY 10003
(212) 533-3500

Neighborhood Map: **Midtown East/Murray Hill**
509 3rd Ave (bet 34th and 35th Sts)
New York, NY 10016
(212) 689-7500

Neighborhood Map: **Upper East Side**
206 E 60th St (bet 2nd and 3rd Aves)
New York, NY 10022
(212) 688-9707

Neighborhood Map: **Upper East Side**
1312 2nd Ave (near 69th St)
New York, NY 10021
(212) 639-1000

Neighborhood Map: **Upper West Side**
61 W 74th St (bet Columbus Ave and Central Park W)
New York, NY 10023
(212) 579-3000

Categories: **Italian, Pizza**
Price Range: **$$**
www.patsyspizzeriany.com

Not to be confused with the original Patsy's in Harlem, this
popular mini-chain of family-friendly pizzerias (with six
locations in Manhattan) specializes in thin-crust pizza (no
slices) and family-style pastas. Full bar. Generally serving
lunch and dinner daily. Hours vary by location.

Zagat: 20 food rating (very good to excellent)

NEW YORK CITY
★TOP100 **Payard Patisserie & Bistro**

★ **BEST DESSERT IN NYC**
1032 Lexington Ave (bet 73rd and 74th Sts)
New York, NY 10021
(212) 717-5252

Neighborhood Map: **Upper East Side**
Categories: **Bakery, Bistro, Dessert, French**

Price Range: **$$$**
www.payard.com

Opened in 1997 by François Payard, now considered among the best pastry chefs in the world, PP&B is a two-in-one landmark of high-end pastry/coffee shop and fine-dining restaurant. Bedecked with inlaid mosaic floors, enormous mirrors and beautiful grand columns holding stately, balloon-shaped light sconces, Payard looks and feels decidedly European. And that's appropriate, as chef Payard, who also has restaurants in Brazil, Japan and Las Vegas, is a third-generation pastry chef born in Nice, France. The front of the house is like the Tiffany's of pastries and chocolate, where a gentleman calling you "madam" or "sir" is likely to escort you to the counter to place your order. Afterwards he will see that your delectable, hand-made sweets — miniature, edible works of art — arrive promptly at your table. The back of the house is the bistro, where Payard handles the dessert menu and chef Phillippe Bertineau does the rest. Multiple menu options are available: prix fixe lunch, standard lunch, tea, dinner pre-theater, dinner tasting, standard dinner and dessert. Entrées include braised Jamison Farm lamb shank with seasonal bean casserole; sautéed East Coast halibut with classic ratatouille, bean and herb salad; and Black Angus hanger steak with house-made French fries and Béarnaise sauce. Full bar. Serving lunch and dinner Mon–Sat. Tea Mon–Sat 3:30 pm–5 pm. Closed Sun.

The New York Times: ★★ (very good); Top Pick
New York magazine: ★★ (very good); Critics' Pick
Zagat: 23 food rating (very good to excellent)
Time Out New York: Critics' Pick
The Village Voice: Critics' Pick

Pearl Oyster Bar

★ **BEST SEAFOOD IN GREENWICH VILLAGE**

18 Cornelia St (bet Bleecker and W 4th Sts)
New York, NY 10014
(212) 691-8211

Neighborhood Map: **Greenwich Village**
Categories: **Oysters, Seafood**
Price Range: **$$$**
www.pearloysterbar.com

This casual, New England-style seafood joint stakes its claim

166

as home to the city's best lobster roll. Beer and wine available. Serving lunch Mon–Fri, dinner Mon–Sat. Closed Sun.

The New York Times: Top Pick
New York magazine: ★★ (very good); Critics' Pick
Zagat: 26 food rating (extraordinary to perfection)
Time Out New York: Critics' Pick
The Village Voice: Critics' Pick

Peasant

194 Elizabeth St (near Spring St)
New York, NY 10012
(212) 965-9511

Neighborhood Map: **Little Italy/NoLita**
Category: **Italian**
Price Range: **$$$**
www.peasantnyc.com

In contrast to the bustle (or hassle, rather) of Little Italy dining, Peasant is a warm, comfortable space distinguished by its wood-burning oven, open kitchen and brick walls. Frank De Carlo's straightforward rustic Italian dishes appear on the menu only in Italian, but your server will gladly assist with translation. Full bar. Serving dinner Tue–Sun.

The New York Times: ★ (good); Top Pick
New York magazine: ★★ (very good); Critics' Pick
Zagat: 24 food rating (very good to excellent)
Time Out New York: Critics' Pick

NEW YORK CITY
★TOP100 Per Se

10 Columbus Cir, 4th Fl (near 60th St, Time Warner Center)
New York, NY 10019
(212) 823-9335

Neighborhood Map: **Midtown West/Theater District**
Category: **Contemporary**
Price Range: **$$$$$**
www.perseny.com

After earning an almost Pavlovian response to his name following the mammoth success of his Yountville, Calif., mecca of French-inspired American dining, Thomas Keller revealed to eager gourmands that his 2004 Manhattan venture would not be a second French Laundry, "per se." Fortunately, however, he brought more than just the signature blue door and Napa Valley serenity to the fourth floor of the Time Warner Center: A live, flat-screen, kitchen-to-kitchen feed is the epicurean nexus between two of the best restaurants in the world. At Per Se, which overlooks Central Park, two nightly nine-course tasting menus showcase an emotional journey through seasonally sublime, high-concept tastes. The signature "Oysters and Pearls" (sabayon of pearl tapioca, Island Creek oysters and Sterling white sturgeon caviar) illustrates the way luxury foods should be consumed, but even simpler dishes — such as marinated summer squash with heirloom tomatoes and arugula with a divine tomato vinaigrette — are an epiphany of flavor and perfection. This Michelin three-star establishment requires reservations two months in advance. Jacket required for lunch and dinner. Full bar. Serving lunch Fri–Sun, dinner nightly.

Michelin Guide: ★ ★★ (exceptional cuisine and worth the journey)
The New York Times: ★★★★ (extraordinary); Top Pick
New York magazine: ★★★★ (exceptional; consistently elite)
Zagat: 28 food rating (extraordinary to perfection)
Time Out New York: Critics' Pick

168

Perry St

★ BEST CONTEMPORARY IN THE WEST VILLAGE/ MEATPACKING DISTRICT

176 Perry St (bet Washington St and 10th Ave)
New York, NY 10014
(212) 352-1900

Neighborhood Map: **West Village/Meatpacking District**
Categories: **Brunch, Contemporary**
Price Range: **$$$**
www.jean-georges.com

More relaxed and invitingly straightforward than many of Jean-Georges Vongerichten's successes, Perry St's exceptional Asian-inspired contemporary dishes fit perfectly in the restaurant's serene setting. Full bar. Serving lunch Mon–Fri, dinner nightly, late-night Thu–Sat. Sat–Sun brunch 11:30 am–3:30 pm.

Michelin Guide: ★ (a very good restaurant in its category)
The New York Times: ★★★ (excellent); Top Pick

New York magazine: ★★ (very good); Critics' Pick
Zagat: 26 food rating (extraordinary to perfection)
The Village Voice: Critics' Pick

NEW YORK CITY **★TOP100** Peter Luger Steak House

★ **BEST STEAK HOUSE IN NYC**

178 Broadway (near Driggs Ave)
Brooklyn, NY 11211
(718) 387-7400

Neighborhood Map: **Brooklyn (Williamsburg)**
Category: **Steak House**
Price Range: **$$$$$**
www.peterluger.com

Peter Luger shines as the Vatican City of all things red
and beefy. Twice-a-week customer Sol Forman purchased
America's sovereign steak house in 1950, and Forman family
members have since been the only ones trusted with the
exacting task of purchasing the 10 tons of beef consumed
under their roof per week. A dining party's only decision here
— aside from, perhaps, choosing between divine creamed
spinach or signature German fried potatoes — is how many
servings of prime porterhouse to split. After dry-aging the
finest cuts in-house for a highly secretive amount of time, the
Luger team butchers, barely sizzles and even slices steaks for
their guests. Pretty much the only thing Peter Luger will allow
diners is to enjoy each precious bite. Reservations required.
Full bar. Cash only. Serving lunch and dinner daily.

Michelin Guide: ★ (a very good restaurant in its category)
The New York Times: ★★ (very good); Top Pick
New York magazine: ★★ (very good); Critics' Pick
Zagat: 27 food rating (extraordinary to perfection)

Petite Crevette

144 Union St (ent on Hicks, bet Union and President Sts)
Brooklyn, NY 11231
(718) 855-2632

Neighborhood Map: **Brooklyn (Carroll Gardens)**
Category: **Seafood**
Price Range: **$$**

This teeny tiny seafood spot offers some of Brooklyn's best (and freshest) seafood. No alcohol available. BYOB. Cash only. Serving lunch Mon–Sat, dinner nightly.

New York magazine: Critics' Pick
Zagat: 24 food rating (very good to excellent)

Pho Viet Huong

★ **BEST VIETNAMESE IN CHINATOWN**

73 Mulberry St (bet Canal and Bayard Sts)
New York, NY 10013
(212) 233-8988

Neighborhood Map: **Chinatown**
Category: **Vietnamese**
Price Range: **$$**

The huge menu is filled with delectable Vietnamese specialties, and this spot is a nice break from the crowds of Chinatown. Beer and wine available. Serving lunch and dinner daily.

Zagat: 22 food rating (very good to excellent)
The Village Voice: Critics' Pick

Piano Due

151 W 51st St (near 7th Ave)
New York, NY 10019
(212) 399-9400

Neighborhood Map: **Midtown West/Theater District**
Category: **Italian**
Price Range: **$$$**

Splurge-worthy Italian specialties are the hallmark of this elegant Midtown Manhattan restaurant with an extensive selection of Italian wines. Reservations suggested. Full bar. Serving lunch Mon–Fri, dinner Mon–Sat. Closed Sun.

New York magazine: Critics' Pick
Zagat: 25 food rating (very good to excellent)

Piccolo Angolo

★ **BEST ITALIAN IN THE WEST VILLAGE/MEATPACKING DISTRICT**

621 Hudson St (near Jane St)
New York, NY 10014
(212) 229-9177

Neighborhood Map: **West Village/Meatpacking District**
Category: **Italian**
Price Range: **$$$**
www.piccoloangolo.com

With a charming setting and divine fare to match, this traditional Italian eatery should not be missed in the New York City tour of Italian restaurants. Beer and wine available. Serving dinner nightly.

Zagat: 25 food rating (very good to excellent)

NEW YORK CITY
★TOP100 Picholine

★ **BEST MEDITERRANEAN ON THE UPPER WEST SIDE**

171

35 W 64th St (bet Broadway and Central Park W)
New York, NY 10023
(212) 724-8585

Neighborhood Map: **Upper West Side**
Categories: **French, Mediterranean**
Price Range: **$$$$$**
www.picholinenyc.com

Considered one of the best restaurants around Lincoln Center and popular with the opera crowd, Picholine is named for the small, green Mediterranean olive and has been praised by the likes of legendary food writer Ruth Reichl, who once wrote in *The New York Times* that the restaurant's menu evinces a "ferocious commitment to quality and the restless inventiveness of its chef-owner, Terrance Brennan." Folks flock here for the French-Mediterranean offerings such as grilled tuna niçoise with tomato jam, tapenade and zucchini flower tempura or the summer-menu prelude of watermelon carpaccio with goat feta parfait, olive salt and *bagna cauda*. There is also a whole-table tasting menu as well as tasting flights and cheese and wine flights. The dining rooms have improved measurably with a series of updates since Picholine

opened in 1993, though you're unlikely to find exceptional ambiance here, what with windowless rooms, plum-colored commercial-style carpeting, lavender walls and seashell-shaped lamps. Still, what the place lacks in *Architectural Digest* chops it more than compensates for with the culinary kind. Jacket suggested for main dining room. Full bar. Serving dinner nightly.

Michelin Guide: ★★ (excellent cooking and worth a detour)
The New York Times: ★★★ (excellent); Top Pick
New York magazine: ★★★★ (exceptional; consistently elite); Critics' Pick
Zagat: 26 food rating (extraordinary to perfection)
Time Out New York: Critics' Pick

Pinche Taqueria

227 Mott St (near Spring St)
New York, NY 10012
(212) 625-0090

Neighborhood Map: **Little Italy/NoLita**
Category: **Mexican**
Price Range: **$**
www.pinchetaqueria.com

With standout fish tacos and organic salsas and tortillas made in-house daily (no microwaves, freezers or canned foods), Pinche Taqueria has thrown its sombrero in the ring in the race for the best and most authentic tacos in town. Beer and wine available. Serving lunch and dinner daily, late-night Fri–Sat.

The Village Voice: Critics' Pick

Po

Neighborhood Map: **Brooklyn (Carroll Gardens)**
276 Smith St (bet Degraw and Sackett Sts)
Brooklyn, NY 11231
(718) 875-1980

Neighborhood Map: **Greenwich Village**
31 Cornelia St (bet Bleecker and W 4th Sts)
New York, NY 10014 (212) 645-2189

Category: **Italian**

Price Range: **$$**
www.porestaurant.com

No longer affiliated with founding partner Mario Batali,
Po continues to succeed with affordable and delicious
Italian cuisine in a romantic setting. The six-course tasting
menu is a steal. Reservations suggested. Beer and wine
available. Serving lunch Wed–Sun, dinner nightly.

The New York Times: Top Pick
Zagat: 24 food rating (very good to excellent)

Posto

★ **BEST PIZZA IN GRAMERCY/MADISON PARK**
310 2nd Ave (near 18th St)
New York, NY 10003
(212) 716-1200

Neighborhood Map: **Gramercy/Madison Park**
Categories: **Italian, Pizza**
Price Range: **$$**
www.postothincrust.com

173

This small, family-friendly pizzeria serves ultra-affordable
and ultra-thin-crust pies amid wooden booths and blue slate
tables. Beer and wine available. Serving lunch and dinner daily,
late-night Fri–Sat.

Zagat: 23 food rating (very good to excellent)

NEW YORK CITY **★TOP100** Prune

★ **BEST BRUNCH IN THE EAST VILLAGE/NOHO**
54 E 1st St (bet 1st and 2nd Aves)
New York, NY 10003
(212) 677-6221

Neighborhood Map: **East Village/NoHo**
Categories: **Brunch, Contemporary**
Price Range: **$$$**
www.prunerestaurant.com

Gotham needs a hero, but this one doesn't wear a cape, fight
crime or carry a grappling hook (that we know of). Instead, this

super woman saves New Yorkers from uninspired, overpriced meals, and she still finds time to raise two children under her alias, Gabrielle Hamilton. The chef/owner's personal touch really shines at Prune (her childhood nickname), as the small dining room has many quirky touches, and the menu reflects her favorite foods growing up. The food is delightfully funky and as progressive as you'll find anywhere in the city, but without the fussiness, pretention or haphazard global accents that often come with contemporary cuisine. For lunch, Prune serves a bacon and marmalade sandwich as well as a hamburger on an English muffin, while dinner features innard-tastic offerings such as roasted marrow bones and the self-proclaimed best sweetbreads in the country, which are fried and topped with bacon and capers. Brunch draws high marks and big crowds clamoring for Bloody Marys — Prune has more than 10 varieties — Dutch pancakes and oyster omelets. Reservations suggested. Full bar. Serving lunch Mon–Fri, dinner nightly. Sat–Sun brunch 10 am–3:30 pm.

The New York Times: ★ (good); Top Pick
New York magazine: ★ (good); Critics' Pick
Zagat: 24 food rating (very good to excellent)
Time Out New York: Critics' Pick

174

Public

★ **BEST CONTEMPORARY IN LITTLE ITALY/NOLITA**

210 Elizabeth St (bet Spring and Prince Sts)
New York, NY 10012
(212) 343-7011

Neighborhood Map: **Little Italy/NoLita**
Categories: **Brunch, Contemporary**
Price Range: **$$$**
www.public-nyc.com

This hip, upscale restaurant calls its cuisine "free-spirited fusion." Reservations suggested. Full bar. Serving dinner nightly, late-night Fri–Sat. Sat–Sun brunch 11 am–3:30 pm.

Michelin Guide: ★ (a very good restaurant in its category)
The New York Times: ★ (good)
New York magazine: Critics' Pick
Zagat: 22 food rating (very good to excellent)
Time Out New York: Critics' Pick

Pure Food and Wine

★ **BEST VEGETARIAN IN UNION SQUARE/FLATIRON**

54 Irving Pl (near 17th St)
New York, NY 10003
(212) 477-1010

Neighborhood Map: **Union Square/Flatiron**
Categories: **Contemporary, Vegetarian**
Price Range: **$$$**
www.purefoodandwine.com

At the forefront of the raw food movement, Pure Food and
Wine serves exclusively vegan and uncooked food (no ovens
in the house). The "limitations" inspire creative, artfully
prepared and innovative dishes. Reservations suggested.
Beer, wine and sake available. Serving dinner nightly.

New York magazine: ★ (good); Critics' Pick
Zagat: 23 food rating (very good to excellent)
Time Out New York: Critics' Pick

Pylos

175

★ **BEST GREEK IN THE EAST VILLAGE/NOHO**

128 E 7th St (bet 1st Ave and Ave A)
New York, NY 10009
(212) 473-0220

Neighborhood Map: **East Village/NoHo**
Categories: **Brunch, Greek**
Price Range: **$$$**
www.pylosrestaurant.com

Named for the clay pots bearing depictions of daily life in the
Hellenic world, Pylos draws acclaim for its rustic Greek cooking
under the direction of consulting chef/cookbook author Diane
Kochilas. Beer and wine available. Serving lunch Wed–Fri,
dinner and late-night nightly. Sat–Sun brunch 11:30 am–4 pm.

The New York Times: ★ (good); Top Pick
Zagat: 25 food rating (very good to excellent)

Queen Restaurant

84 Court St (bet Livingston and Schermerhorn Sts)

Brooklyn, NY 11201
(718) 596-5954

Neighborhood Map: **Brooklyn (Brooklyn Heights)**
Category: **Italian**
Price Range: **$$**
www.queenrestaurant.com

Family-owned and -operated for 50 years, Queen serves
white-tablecloth Italian fare that's fit for a monarch.
Reservations suggested. Full bar. Serving lunch Mon–Fri,
dinner nightly.

Zagat: 24 food rating (very good to excellent)

NEW YORK CITY
★TOP100 Raoul's

★ **BEST BISTRO IN SOHO**

180 Prince St (bet Sullivan and Thompson Sts)
New York, NY 10012
(212) 966-3518

Neighborhood Map: **SoHo**
Categories: **Bistro, Contemporary, French**
Price Range: **$$$**
www.raouls.com

The history of Raoul's is the stuff of neighborhood restaurant
dreams. In 1975, two poor Alsatian brothers bought a speakeasy-
like space in SoHo, and, through little more than perseverance
and word of mouth, transformed it into one of the longest-lasting
and most beloved (reservations are a must) French bistros in
town. Though it may be a bit pricey for today's cash-strapped
creatives, a fashionable, Euro-centric crowd still packs the main
dining room that retains the laid-back, sexy bistro ambiance
of its early days: dark lighting, tin ceilings, chalkboard menus,
black booths and art covered walls — for what it's worth, Martin
Scorsese found the place compelling enough to use in a scene
for *The Departed*. The French fare is classic and hearty, from the
ever-popular rendition of steak au poivre to rack of lamb or the
oysters du jour. Raoul's isn't progressive, but people love it, in
part because it's changed so little over the years. Reservations
suggested. Full bar. Serving dinner and late-night nightly.

Zagat: 23 food rating (very good to excellent)
Time Out New York: Critics' Pick

The Red Cat

★ **BEST CONTEMPORARY IN CHELSEA**

227 10th Ave (bet 23rd and 24th Sts)
New York, NY 10011
(212) 242-1122

Neighborhood Map: **Chelsea**
Categories: **Contemporary, Mediterranean**
Price Range: **$$**
www.theredcat.com

Best classified as contemporary Mediterranean cuisine, Chelsea's Red Cat, a rising star among Manhattan's most progressive restaurants, knows no boundaries with its eclectic and delicious fare. Bacon tempura anyone? Reservations suggested. Full bar. Serving lunch Tue–Sat, dinner nightly, late-night Fri–Sat.

The New York Times: ★★ (very good); Top Pick
New York magazine: Critics' Pick
Zagat: 24 food rating (very good to excellent)
Time Out New York: Critics' Pick

177

Relish

225 Wythe Ave (near N 3rd St)
Brooklyn, NY 11211
(718) 963-4546

Neighborhood Map: **Brooklyn (Williamsburg)**
Categories: **American Traditional, Brunch**
Price Range: **$$**
www.relish.com

This honest-to-goodness steel diner car in Williamsburg houses "New American" specialties. Full bar. Serving lunch, dinner and late-night daily. Sat–Sun brunch.

The New York Times: Top Pick
Zagat: 20 food rating (very good to excellent)
Time Out New York: Critics' Pick

Republic

★ **BEST ASIAN FUSION IN UNION SQUARE/FLATIRON**

37 Union Sq W (bet 16th and 17th Sts)
New York, NY 10003
(212) 627-7172

Neighborhood Map: **Union Square/Flatiron**
Categories: **Asian Fusion, Chinese, Noodle House, Thai**
Price Range: **$$**
www.thinknoodles.com

This minimalist, ultra-modern eatery encourages you to "think noodles: fresh, fast and affordable." Try the glass noodles or vermicelli noodles with shredded duck. Full bar. Serving lunch and dinner daily.

The New York Times: Top Pick
New York magazine: Critics' Pick
Zagat: 18 food rating (good to very good)

Resto

111 E 29th St (bet Park and Lexington Aves)
New York, NY 10016
(212) 685-5585

Neighborhood Map: **Gramercy/Madison Park**
Categories: **Belgian, Brunch**
Price Range: **$$$**
www.restonyc.com

Billing itself as a "laid-back neighborhood gathering place with approachable Belgian food in the style of New York," Resto offers feasts of whole pig or lamb for groups with advance reservations. Reservations suggested. Full bar. Serving lunch Mon–Fri, dinner nightly, late-night Thu–Sat. Sat–Sun brunch 10:30 am–3 pm.

The New York Times: ★ ★ (very good); Top Pick
New York magazine: Critics' Pick
Zagat: 20 food rating (very good to excellent)

Rice 'n' Beans
★ **BEST LATIN/SOUTH AMERICAN IN MIDTOWN WEST/ THEATER DISTRICT**

744 9th Ave (near 50th St)
New York, NY 10019

(212) 265-4444

Neighborhood Map: **Midtown West/Theater District**
Categories: **Brunch, Latin/South American**
Price Range: **$$**
www.ricenbeansrestaurant.com

The name doesn't quite say it all here, as the menu contains
many tasty fish, chicken and beef dishes. Brazilian specialty
rice and beans are deliciously paired with each entrée. Beer
and wine available. Serving lunch and dinner daily.

The New York Times: Top Pick
Zagat: 22 food rating (very good to excellent)

Rigoletto Pizza

★ BEST PIZZA ON THE UPPER WEST SIDE

208 Columbus Ave (bet 69th and 70th Sts)
New York, NY 10023
(212) 721-2929

Neighborhood Map: **Upper West Side**
Category: **Pizza**
Price Range: **$$**

Strapped for cash after shelling out some dough for opera
tickets at Lincoln Center? Ignore the myriad pre-theater
bistros nearby and try the best thin-crust pizza on the Upper
West Side at Rigoletto, open since 1991. No alcohol available.
Serving lunch and dinner daily.

NEW YORK CITY **★TOP100** The River Café

1 Water St (near Broadway)
Brooklyn, NY 11201
(718) 522-5200

Neighborhood Map: **Brooklyn (Dumbo)**
Categories: **Brunch, Contemporary**
Price Range: **$$$$$**
www.rivercafe.com

In the classiest possible way, Brooklyn's River Café screams
special-occasion restaurant. There's a stunning view of

both the river and the Manhattan skyline, a small army of tuxedo-clad servers, and a pianist to provide the dinner's accompaniment. Plus a slew of now-celebrity chefs sharpened their skills here over the course of its 30-year history. Lunch is served à la carte, while dinner features three- or six-course prix fixe options. The cuisine is of classic fine-dining caliber: You won't come across the most progressive dishes in town, but why mess with success when traditional offerings such as rack of lamb, prime-aged sirloin, crisp duck breast and lobster never fail to impress? As your memorable meal comes to an end, take in the view of the Brooklyn Bridge, and then literally take it in (i.e., ingest) — the Chocolate Marquise Brooklyn Bridge tastily replicates this landmark. Jacket required in the main dining room and main bar after 5 pm. Reservations required. Full bar with an extensive wine list. Serving lunch Mon–Sat, dinner nightly. Prix fixe Sun brunch 11 am–3 pm.

The New York Times: ★★ (very good); Top Pick
Zagat: 26 food rating (extraordinary to perfection)
Time Out New York: Critics' Pick

NEW YORK CITY
★TOP100 Rosa Mexicano

★ **BEST MEXICAN IN MIDTOWN EAST/MURRAY HILL**
Neighborhood Map: **Midtown East/Murray Hill**
1063 1st Ave (near 58th St)
New York, NY 10022
(212) 753-7407

★ **BEST MEXICAN IN UNION SQUARE/FLATIRON**
Neighborhood Map: **Union Square/Flatiron**
9 E 18th St (near 5th Ave)
New York, NY 10003
(212) 533-3350

★ **BEST MEXICAN ON THE UPPER WEST SIDE**
Neighborhood Map: **Upper West Side**
61 Columbus Ave (near 62nd St)
New York, NY 10023
(212) 977-7700

Categories: **Brunch, Contemporary, Mexican**
Price Range: **$$**
www.rosamexicano.info

With three convenient locations in the city (Lincoln Center, Union Square, First Avenue at 58th Street), New Yorkers have no excuse not to guac out at one of these wildly popular margar-eateries. Upscale Mexican is the order of the day, and their oft-imitated, legendary guacamole prepared tableside along with colorful frozen pomegranate margaritas draw families and young happy-hour goers alike. Bright colors, the trademark shimmering blue water wall, and windows with beaded curtains forming rose patterns set the celebratory tone. Corn tortillas are made on-site and provide the foundation for wild mushroom quesadillas and crabmeat enchiladas with pumpkin seeds and tomatillo sauce. Tacos — with fillings from ancho-marinated chicken to tender goat with poblano peppers — are served in a cast iron skillet and accentuated with fresh salsas such as the green habanera-garlic. Mexican chocolate and raspberry rose ice cream provide sophisticated flavors and a sweet finish to any meal. Given the crowds that have consistently packed the place since the first location opened in 1984, it's no wonder that Rosa Mexicano has expanded to Atlanta, Palm Beach, Miami and the nation's capital. Reservations suggested. Full bar. Lincoln Center and Union Square serving lunch Mon–Fri, dinner nightly. Sat–Sun brunch. First Avenue serving dinner nightly.

Zagat: 21 food rating (very good to excellent)
The Village Voice: Critics' Pick

Russ & Daughters

★ **BEST GOURMET TAKEOUT ON THE LOWER EAST SIDE**

179 E Houston St (bet Orchard and Allen Sts)
New York, NY 10002
(212) 475-4880

Neighborhood Map: **Lower East Side**
Categories: **Bakery, Deli, Gourmet Takeout**
Price Range: **$**
www.russanddaughters.com

Since 1914, New Yorkers have been coming here for some of the city's best kosher-style eats. The smoked fish selection is legendary. No alcohol available. Serving during breakfast, lunch and early dinner hours daily.

Sable's

★ **BEST DELI ON THE UPPER EAST SIDE**

1489 2nd Ave (bet 77th and 78th Sts)
New York, NY 10075
(212) 249-6177

Neighborhood Map: **Upper East Side**
Categories: **Breakfast, Deli, Gourmet Takeout,
    Seafood**
Price Range: **$**
www.sablesnyc.com

Boasting "the world's best smoked salmon, sturgeon and
caviar," this market also offers a nice selection of hot and
cold sandwiches (for dine-in or takeout). No alcohol available.
Serving breakfast, lunch and dinner daily.

NEW YORK CITY
★TOP100 Saigon Grill

★ **BEST VIETNAMESE IN NYC**

Neighborhood Map: **Greenwich Village**
93 University Pl (bet 11th and 12th Sts)
New York, NY 10003
(212) 982-3691

Neighborhood Map: **Upper West Side**
620 Amsterdam Ave (near 90th St)
New York, NY 10024
(212) 875-9072

Category: **Vietnamese**
Price Range: **$$**

A popular choice because of bountiful portions and budget-
friendly prices, Saigon Grill boasts locations in Greenwich
Village and the Upper West Side. Décor is limited, and lighting
dark, but the extensive menu showcasing flavors of Vietnam
excuses the functional dining rooms. You may have to fight the
crowds, but food arrives moments after ordering, so turnover
is quick. The city is becoming more and more noodle-centric,
and these menus feature plenty to choose from, with *bun xao*
(stir-fried rice noodles with shredded vegetables, crushed
peanuts, and egg), *bun* (room temperature rice vermicelli
with cucumber, peanut, fresh herbs and *nuoc chom* sauce)
and *banh hoi* (steamed angel hair noodles). All come with

choice of meat. Other dishes include shrimp summer rolls, a number of soups, curries and seafood specialties, and the Spicy Beef Saigon Style, with hot peppers, shiitake mushrooms and asparagus. Vegetarian options abound, and don't neglect some sweet rice dumplings for dessert. Full bar. Serving lunch, dinner and late-night daily.

Zagat: 21 food rating (very good to excellent)

Sakagura

211 E 43rd St, B1F (bet 2nd and 3rd Aves)
New York, NY 10017
(212) 953-7253

Neighborhood Map: **Midtown East/Murray Hill**
Category: **Japanese/Sushi**
Price Range: **$$**

You'll feel like you've made a major discovery as you enter Sakagura, hidden in the basement of a Midtown office building. Sake bottles lining the walls and delicious house-made soba noodles give Sakagura the look, and taste, of Tokyo. It's known nationwide as a top-notch sake bar. Beer, wine and sake available. Serving lunch Mon–Fri, dinner nightly, late-night Fri–Sat.

The New York Times: Top Pick
Zagat: 25 food rating (very good to excellent)

183

NEW YORK CITY
★TOP100 Sarabeth's

★ **BEST BRUNCH IN NYC**
Neighborhood Map: **Chelsea**
75 9th Ave (near 15th St)
New York, NY 10011
(212) 989-2424

Neighborhood Map: **Midtown West/Theater District**
40 Central Park S (bet 5th and 6th Aves)
New York, NY 10019
(212) 826-5959

Neighborhood Map: **Upper East Side**
1295 Madison Ave (near 92nd St)

New York, NY 10128
(212) 410-7335

Neighborhood Map: **Upper East Side**
945 Madison Ave (near 75th St, The Whitney)
New York, NY 10021
(212) 570-3670

Neighborhood Map: **Upper West Side**
423 Amsterdam Ave (near 80th St)
New York, NY 10024
(212) 496-6280

Categories: **American Traditional, Bakery, Breakfast, Brunch**
Price Range: **$$**
www.sarabeth.com

Why wait an hour and a half for brunch when you can walk right in across the street? Because there is comfort food — and then there is Sarabeth's. Originally opened in 1981 as an Upper West Side retail shop offering baked goods and homemade jam, Sarabeth's eventually answered the demands of her customers and began a restaurant service, most notably a menu of breakfast standards such as eggs Benedict, omelets, French toast, waffles and pancakes that she executes brilliantly. But while Sarabeth's may be most famous for its ultimate breakfast-and-lunch fare — not to mention a prolific offering of shamefully decadent baked goods — several locations in her growing empire also serve dinner (the only meal for which reservations are accepted). Amid an atmosphere that is homey but decidedly classy, the dinner menu includes appetizers such as roasted beet salad with pears and entrées such as free-range chicken potpie. We would bet the ranch on her any day in a Sarabeth v. Paula Deen smackdown, from which Paula would no doubt emerge thumped, dejected and covered in flour. The Amsterdam Avenue location features a full bar and serves breakfast, lunch, tea and dinner daily. Call other locations for hours.

The New York Times: Top Pick
Zagat: 20 food rating (very good to excellent)

Saravanaas

★ **BEST VEGETARIAN IN GRAMERCY/MADISON PARK**
81 Lexington Ave (near 26th St)

184

New York, NY 10016
(212) 679-0204

Neighborhood Map: **Gramercy/Madison Park**
Categories: **Breakfast, Indian, Vegetarian**
Price Range: **$**

This restaurant offers exclusively vegetarian fare, including seasoned *dosas*, lentil cakes and mung-bean-and-vegetable stew. Reservations suggested. Beer and wine available. Serving breakfast, lunch and dinner daily.

The New York Times: Top Pick
New York magazine: Critics' Pick
Zagat: 24 food rating (very good to excellent)

Sarge's Deli

548 3rd Ave (bet 36th and 37th Sts)
New York, NY 10016
(212) 679-0442

Neighborhood Map: **Midtown East/Murray Hill**
Categories: **Breakfast, Deli**
Price Range: **$$**

Sarge's serves up its top-notch sandwiches, matzo ball soup and well-known breakfast favorites 24 hours a day. Beer and wine available. Open 24 hours.

Zagat: 18 food rating (good to very good)

Saul

★ **BEST CONTEMPORARY IN BROOKLYN**
140 Smith St (bet Dean and Bergen Sts)
Brooklyn, NY 11201
(718) 935-9844

Neighborhood Map: **Brooklyn (Boerum Hill)**
Category: **Contemporary**
Price Range: **$$$**
www.saulrestaurant.com

Another example of a Brooklyn restaurant giving top-rated Manhattan spots a run for their money, Saul's seasonal,

contemporary cuisine is nothing if not superlative.
Reservations suggested. Full bar. Serving dinner nightly.

Michelin Guide: ★ (a very good restaurant in its category)
The New York Times: Top Pick
New York magazine: Critics' Pick
Zagat: 27 food rating (extraordinary to perfection)

Savoy

★ BEST CONTEMPORARY IN SOHO

70 Prince St (near Crosby St)
New York, NY 10012
(212) 219-8570

Neighborhood Map: **SoHo**
Category: **Contemporary**
Price Range: **$$$**
www.savoynyc.com

Occupying two levels of a charming townhouse in SoHo, Savoy
is serious about sourcing seasonally sustainable ingredients
from local farmers. The street level bar and café accomodates
more casual diners, while dinner in the main dining room on
the second floor features entrées such as Vermont suckling
pig roulade or salt crusted baby duck. Reservations suggested.
Full bar. Serving lunch Mon–Sat, dinner nightly.

The New York Times: ★★ (very good); Top Pick
New York magazine: Critics' Pick
Zagat: 23 food rating (very good to excellent)

Scalini Fedeli

★ BEST ITALIAN IN TRIBECA

165 Duane St (near Hudson St)
New York, NY 10013
(212) 528-0400

Neighborhood Map: **TriBeCa**
Category: **Italian**
Price Range: **$$$$**
www.scalinifedeli.com

The French-influenced Italian menu offers prix fixe and

186

tasting menus in a romantic dining room featuring vaulted ceilings, antiques and Tuscan-inspired art. Full bar. Serving lunch Tue–Fri, dinner Mon–Sat. Closed Sun.

New York magazine: Critics' Pick
Zagat: 27 food rating (extraordinary to perfection

Schiller's Liquor Bar

131 Rivington St (near Norfolk St)
New York, NY 10002
(212) 260-4555

Neighborhood Map: **Lower East Side**
Categories: **American Traditional, Bistro, Breakfast, Brunch**
Price Range: **$$**
www.schillersny.com

A something-for-everyone menu, including French bistro favorites, and a trendy nighttime bar scene make this a go-to neighborhood spot. Reservations suggested. Full bar. Serving breakfast and lunch Mon–Fri, dinner and late-night nightly. Sat–Sun brunch 10 am–5 pm.

187

New York magazine: Critics' Pick
Zagat: 18 food rating (good to very good)
Time Out New York: Critics' Pick

NEW YORK CITY
★TOP100 2nd Ave Deli

★ **BEST DELI IN MIDTOWN EAST/MURRAY HILL**
162 E 33rd St (bet 3rd and Lexington Aves)
New York, NY 10016
(212) 677-0606

Neighborhood Map: **Midtown East/Murray Hill**
Categories: **Breakfast, Deli, Diner, Kosher**
Price Range: **$$**
www.2ndavedeli.com

You know what they say: Even if you're Catholic, you're Jewish if you live in New York. Serving the ultimate in kosher deli food, 2nd Ave Deli is no longer actually on Second Avenue, as the East Village original that opened in 1954 fell victim to rising rents and closed in 2006. This recent reincarnation, run by the original owner's nephew, is on East 33rd Street near Third Avenue and hews closely to its beloved archetype. Every diner is treated to a plate of whole sour pickles and a serving of cold, crisp coleslaw, and the legendary *gribenes* (deep-fried chicken skin topped with chopped onions) remain one of the favorite menu offerings. Other popular dishes include the thick, melt-in-your-mouth, house-cured corned beef, the peppery pastrami, and chicken matzo ball soup. The service is prompt and attentive and may include a shot of chocolate soda at the end of your meal, if you're lucky. Full bar. Serving breakfast, lunch, dinner and late-night daily.

The New York Times: ★ (good); Top Pick

NEW YORK CITY
★TOP100 Sette Mezzo

★ **BEST ITALIAN ON THE UPPER EAST SIDE**
969 Lexington Ave (bet 70th and 71st Sts)
New York, NY 10021
(212) 472-0400

Neighborhood Map: **Upper East Side**
Category: **Italian**
Price Range: **$$$**

An endorsement from Oprah is a license to print money, but this Upper East Side trattoria had already established quite a stately clientele of high rollers about town even before receiving her high praise. Regulars get the regal treatment here. Take a hint from them and bring plenty of cash, as plastic is not accepted. Northern Italian pastas, tender veal cuts and fresh fish (be sure to note the seafood special of the day) populate the menu. The *pollo patanato*, chicken breast encrusted with a thin layer of potato, is a crowd favorite, as are the grilled scallops and artichoke appetizers (Oprah's go-tos). In season, truffles may play an integral part of your meal. The house-made limoncello provides a smooth, sweet finish to a memorable meal. Beer and wine available. Cash only. Serving lunch and dinner daily.

Zagat: 23 food rating (very good to excellent)

Settepani Bakery
Neighborhood Map: **Brooklyn (Williamsburg)**

602 Lorimer St (bet Conselyea St and Skillman Ave)
Brooklyn, NY 11211
(718) 349-6524

Neighborhood Map: **Harlem**
196 Lenox Ave (near 120th St)
New York, NY 10026
(917) 492-4806

Categories: **Bakery, Brunch, Café**
Price Range: **$**
www.settepani.com

With a name like Settepani, literally "seven breads" in Italian, owner Antonio Settepani's calling in life was pretty well determined at birth. These family-owned and -operated Italian bakeries — the flagship bakery is in Brooklyn while a second café (with its more extensive menu, including a weekend brunch) opened in Harlem — churn out a wide variety of breads, pastries, cakes, biscotti and other sweet treats. No alcohol available. Generally serving during breakfast, lunch and dinner hours daily. Call for hours.

189

71 Irving Place Coffee & Tea Bar

★ **BEST COFFEEHOUSE IN UNION SQUARE/FLATIRON**

71 Irving Pl (near 19th St)
New York, NY 10003
(212) 995-5252

Neighborhood Map: **Union Square/Flatiron**
Categories: **Café, Coffeehouse**
Price Range: **$**
www.irvingfarm.com

This cozy café on the ground floor of a historic brownstone brews fresh, estate-grown coffee from Irving Farm and offers pastries and other light fare. Beer and wine available. Serving during breakfast, lunch and dinner hours daily.

New York magazine: Critics' Pick

NEW YORK CITY **★TOP100** Shake Shack

★ **BEST BURGERS IN GRAMERCY/MADISON PARK**

Madison Sq Park (near 23rd St and Madison Ave)
New York, NY 10010
(212) 889-6600

Neighborhood Map: **Gramercy/Madison Park**
Categories: **Burgers, Hot Dogs, Ice Cream**
Price Range: **$**
www.shakeshacknyc.com

A steaming plate of cheese fries and a glass of Shiraz on a
sizzling hot summer day? Why not? The city's best milk shake
on a bitter, blustery January evening? Bring it on. Shake Shack
is now open year-round, which means New Yorkers can enjoy
America's greatest un-health foods no matter the season.
Located in Madison Square Park (with a second location
slated to open on the Upper West Side in late 2008 on the
corner of Columbus Avenue and 77th Street), Shake Shack is
restaurateur extraordinaire Danny Meyer's (Union Square
Cafe, Gramercy Tavern, Blue Smoke, the list goes on) kitschy
tribute to the summery roadside food stand. Since opening
in 2004, it's attracted very long lines for its Chicago-style hot
dogs, concretes (an intensely thick milk shake) and one of
New York's most praised burgers. Though a certain maroon-
covered dining guide may give it a low rating for "décor,"
what environs could possibly be better for a burger, frozen
custard or a beer than the park? Burgers are pretty basic:
cooked medium and served plain with lettuce, tomato, onion,
pickle and cheese upon request. Variations include the double
cheeseburger and even a 'Shroom Burger for the Hacky Sack
crowd. Beer and wine available. Serving lunch and dinner daily.
Hours may vary by season.

The New York Times: Top Pick
New York magazine: Critics' Pick
Zagat: 23 food rating (very good to excellent)

NEW YORK CITY **★TOP100** **Shun Lee Palace**

★ **BEST CHINESE IN NYC**
155 E 55th St (bet Lexington and 3rd Aves)
New York, NY 10022
(212) 371-8844

Neighborhood Map: **Midtown East/Murray Hill**
Categories: **Chinese, Contemporary**
Price Range: **$$$**

http://shunleepalace.lanteck.net

Order in some General Tso's chicken and beef with broccoli from that place on the corner for the kids and a babysitter, and treat yourself to a night out with some deluxe upscale Chinese at Shun Lee Palace. Since 1971, this lush, palatial eatery in Midtown has proven that the best Chinese isn't necessarily found in Chinatown, or in a signless dive, for that matter. The sizable menu borrows from multiple traditions in Chinese cooking and incorporates some contemporary American elements as well in dishes such as Szechwan rack of lamb, sweetbreads with black mushrooms or Cantonese baked lobster. Other standouts include Hunan-style whole sea bass, multiple duck preparations and the Ants Climb on Tree (minced filet stir-fried with cellophane noodles and a spicy garlic sauce). For more bang for your buck, try the prix fixe lunch. A sister location, Shun Lee West near Lincoln Center, has a similar menu with many dim sum offerings. Full bar. Reservations suggested. Serving lunch and dinner daily.

The New York Times: ★★ (very good)
New York magazine: Critics' Pick
Zagat: 24 food rating (very good to excellent)
Time Out New York: Critics' Pick

191

Smith & Wollensky

797 3rd Ave (near 49th St)
New York, NY 10022
(212) 753-1530

Neighborhood Map: **Midtown East/Murray Hill**
Category: **Steak House**
Price Range: **$$$$**
www.smithandwollensky.com

The most trafficked steak joint in New York, this 49th Street mainstay remains the ideal place to exercise the corporate plastic for both turf and surf. The adjacent and more casual Wollensky's Grill stays open until 2 am nightly with an expanded menu. Reservations suggested. Full bar. Serving lunch, dinner and late-night daily.

The New York Times: ★★ (very good)
Zagat: 22 food rating (very good to excellent)
Time Out New York: Critics' Pick

The Smoke Joint

★ **BEST BARBECUE IN BROOKLYN**

87 S Elliot Pl (near Fulton St)
Brooklyn, NY 11217
(718) 797-1011

Neighborhood Map: **Brooklyn (Fort Greene)**
Category: **Barbecue**
Price Range: **$$**
www.thesmokejoint.com

In the competition for best barbecue in New York, The Smoke Joint holds its own, not coincidentally because it smokes its own. Beer and wine available. Serving lunch and dinner daily.

The New York Times: Top Pick
Zagat: 22 food rating (very good to excellent)
The Village Voice: Critics' Pick

Snack

★ **BEST GREEK IN SOHO**

105 Thompson St (bet Prince and Spring Sts)
New York, NY 10012
(212) 925-1040

Neighborhood Map: **SoHo**
Categories: **Greek, Mediterranean, Small Plates**
Price Range: **$$**

Fresh Greek *meze* at very reasonable prices are the mainstay at this tiny SoHo spot, but sandwiches and full-on entrées are also available. Beer and wine available. Serving lunch and dinner daily.

New York magazine: Critics' Pick
Zagat: 22 food rating (very good to excellent)

NEW YORK CITY ★TOP100 Sparks Steak House

★ **BEST STEAK HOUSE IN MIDTOWN EAST/MURRAY HILL**

210 E 46th St (bet 2nd and 3rd Aves)
New York, NY 10017
(212) 687-4855

Neighborhood Map: **Midtown East/Murray Hill**
Category: **Steak House**
Price Range: **$$$$**
www.sparkssteakhouse.com

Established in 1966, Sparks Steak House has quite a colorful history, to put it lightly. It was formerly a popular spot among mob bosses. In fact, the Gambino family put a hit on then-boss Paul Castellano outside the doors in 1985. Thankfully for the average diner, things have calmed down in the world of organized crime, and Sparks draws crowds for the right reasons: its old-school, swanky environs, choice cuts, and impressive wine list. In the great steak house wars of New York City, Sparks ranks among the best and can definitely claim to be the biggest, as this manly meat emporium can seat almost 700. Despite its vastness, you'll likely have to wait for a table, but that's nothing a dry martini can't help you through. The prime sirloin is the best seller, and other classic cuts include extra-thick lamb chops, the steak fromage (with Roquefort cheese) and beef scaloppini. Live lobsters can weigh in at about six pounds, so be forewarned of the pet-sized crustacean that will arrive on your plate. Reservations suggested. Full bar with award-winning wine list. Serving lunch Mon–Fri, dinner Mon–Sat. Closed Sun.

The New York Times: ★ (good)
New York magazine: ★★ (very good); Critics' Pick
Zagat: 25 food rating (very good to excellent)
Time Out New York: Critics' Pick

NEW YORK CITY
★TOP100 Spice Market

★ **BEST ASIAN FUSION IN NYC**
403 W 13th St (near 9th Ave)
New York, NY 10014
(212) 675-2322

Neighborhood Map: **West Village/Meatpacking District**
Category: **Asian Fusion**
Price Range: **$$**
www.spicemarketnewyork.com

Southeast Asian street-food-inspired fare served in a warehouse turned no-luxury-spared palace: If this concept could exist anywhere on earth, it would be the Meatpacking District. In the hands of Jean-Georges Vongerichten, Spice

Market proves to be a wild ride for the tastebuds, not just the eyes. Tapestries, wood-carved pagodas, candles, silk lanterns and a waitstaff dressed as monks set the scene for indulgence, so why not order a specialty cocktail and enjoy the show? The menu consists largely of playful, dressed up renditions of market and street food enjoyed by Vongerichten while he traveled through Ho Chi Minh City, Bangkok and elsewhere in Southeast Asia. Starters include spring rolls, chicken samosas with yogurt, and mussels steamed with lemongrass, coconut juice, dried chili and Thai basil. Entrées such as red curried duck, onion- and chili-crusted short ribs, and steamed lobster with fried garlic, dried chili and ginger are served family-style — the foods of the people in a dining room fit for a king. Reservations suggested. Full bar. Serving lunch, dinner and late-night daily.

The New York Times: ★★★ (excellent); Top Pick
New York magazine: ★★ (very good); Critics' Pick
Zagat: 22 food rating (very good to excellent)
Time Out New York: Critics' Pick

NEW YORK CITY
⭐**TOP100** **The Spotted Pig**

★ **BEST IRISH/BRITISH IN NYC**
314 W 11th St (near Greenwich St)
New York, NY 10014
(212) 620-0393

Neighborhood Map: **West Village/Meatpacking District**
Categories: **Brunch, Burgers, Gastropub, Irish/British**
Price Range: **$$$**
www.thespottedpig.com

Co-owner/chef and British expat April Bloomfield created quite the hot spot with her trendy West Village eatery, proving our English-speaking brethren across the pond have more culinary gems to boast than bangers and mash or steak and kidney pie. A gastropub is generally defined as a drinking establishment with a food problem — plenty of beverages from which to choose and an upscale menu that often steals the show. In this case, there are two cask-conditioned ales, an extensive wine list and excellent cocktails (try the dirty martini). Meanwhile, the Pig's illustrious Michelin star, awarded in 2006, may have attracted the initial crowds, but it's the signature pig's ears, sheep's ricotta *gnudi* (ravioli without the wrapper) and Roquefort-smothered burgers that have kept the scene sparkling and packed to the brim seven nights a week. If crowds aren't your thing, the Cubano sandwich at lunch is a slice of hog heaven in itself. Full bar. Serving lunch, dinner and late-night daily. Sat–Sun brunch 11 am–3 pm.

Michelin Guide: ★ (a very good restaurant in its category)
The New York Times: ★ (good); Top Pick
New York magazine: ★★ (very good); Critics' Pick
Zagat: 22 food rating (very good to excellent)
Time Out New York: Critics' Pick

Strictly Roots

★ **BEST VEGETARIAN IN HARLEM**
2058 Adam Clayton Powell Jr Blvd (near 123rd St)
New York, NY 10027
(212) 864-8699

Neighborhood Map: **Harlem**
Categories: **Breakfast, Buffet/Cafeteria, Caribbean/ Tropical, Soul Food, Vegetarian**
Price Range: **$**

Locals line up at this small, colorful Harlem eatery for its unique brand of vegetarian and vegan "soul food" with a heavy Caribbean influence. No alcohol available. BYOB. Serving breakfast Mon–Fri, lunch and dinner daily.

Sugiyama

251 W 55th St (bet Broadway and 8th Ave)
New York, NY 10019
(212) 956-0670

Neighborhood Map: **Midtown West/Theater District**
Category: **Japanese/Sushi**
Price Range: **$$$**
www.sugiyama-nyc.com

Offering a prix fixe menu, and specials for pre- and post-theater goers, chef Nao Sugiyama specializes in authentic kaiseki-style Japanese fare served in a natural, serene dining room. Reservations suggested. Beer, wine and sake available. Serving dinner Tue–Sat. Closed Sun–Mon.

The New York Times: ★★★ (excellent)

195

New York magazine: Critics' Pick
Zagat: 27 food rating (extraordinary to perfection)

Super Tacos (taco truck)

96th St and Broadway
New York, NY 10025
(917) 837-0866

Neighborhood Map: **Upper West Side**
Categories: **Food Cart, Mexican**
Price Range: **$**

Street meat aficionados flock to this taco truck on 96th and Broadway. Don't be afraid of a little tongue taco, and wash it all down with an *horchata*. No alcohol available. Serving lunch Sat–Sun, dinner and late-night nightly.

NEW YORK CITY ★TOP100 Sushi of Gari

Neighborhood Map: **Midtown West/Theater District**
347 W 46th St (bet 8th and 9th Aves)
New York, NY 10036
(212) 957-0046

★ **BEST JAPANESE/SUSHI ON THE UPPER EAST SIDE**
Neighborhood Map: **Upper East Side**
402 E 78th St (bet York and 1st Aves)
New York, NY 10021
(212) 517-5340

★ **BEST JAPANESE/SUSHI ON THE UPPER WEST SIDE**
Neighborhood Map: **Upper West Side**
370 Columbus Ave (near 77th St)
New York, NY 10024
(212) 362-4816

Category: **Japanese/Sushi**
Price Range: **$$$**
www.sushiofgari.com

When it comes to sushi-eating etiquette, the customer is not always right at Sushi of Gari. This tiny Upper East Side haven for sashimi devotees perfectly sauces the fish before it arrives on your plate and withholds soy sauce and wasabi in a noble attempt to prevent diners from drowning the fresh flavor in a sea of soy sauce. Chef Masatoshi "Gari" Sugio, who enjoys a bit of a cult following for his contributions to the avant-garde sushi movement, has been preparing sushi since age 17, so why not trust the chef with the popular *omakase* (literal translation: trust), a selection of the best seasonal fish cuts of the day. Both raw and slightly cooked offerings are innovative and accentuated by Gari's signature sauces, from bluefin tuna with ponzu mousse or the Japanese red snapper salad to "torched" squid with sea urchin sauce. For dessert, there's tempura ice cream. Newer locations include Gari on the Upper West Side and Gari 46 in the theater district. Beer, wine and sake available. Sushi of Gari and Gari serving dinner Tue–Sun. Closed Mon. Gari 46 serving dinner nightly.

Michelin Guide: ★ (a very good restaurant in its category)
The New York Times: ★★ (very good); Top Pick
New York magazine: ★★★ (generally excellent); Critics' Pick
Zagat: 26 food rating (extraordinary to perfection)

NEW YORK CITY
★**TOP100** Sushi Yasuda

★ **BEST JAPANESE/SUSHI IN NYC**

204 E 43rd St (bet 2nd and 3rd Aves)
New York, NY 10017
(212) 972-1001

Neighborhood Map: **Midtown East/Murray Hill**
Category: **Japanese/Sushi**
Price Range: **$$$**
www.sushiyasuda.com

For the owners and sushi chefs here, this place is less a restaurant and more a calling — an institution whose mission of serving some of the best sushi in New York City demands unwavering discipline and attention to every conceivable detail, right down to the twice-daily cleaning (with unprocessed rice bran) of the tables and sushi counter, which chef Naomichi Yasuda helped build by hand. The mix of Japanese short- and medium-grain rice is made in-house every morning, and there is no Kikkoman soy sauce to be found here. No, they make their own, and they advise that customers use it sparingly so as not to diminish the taste of the famously fresh fish. The sushi chefs also instruct against mixing wasabi directly into the soy sauce, encouraging you to add a small amount directly on the fish instead. The beautiful dining room of solid bamboo planks draws the Midtown business crowd (at lunch in particular), creative types from downtown, and everybody in between. Chef Yasuda prides himself on customizing each meal, and is even said to consider the size of his patrons' mouths before preparing their sushi. *The New York Times* food critic Frank Bruni recommends going with only one other person, as opposed to a group, as "the men in white and first-rate fish they're cutting give you all the company and diversion you need." Reservations suggested. Beer, wine and sake available. Serving lunch Mon–Fri, dinner Mon–Sat. Closed Sun.

The New York Times: ★★★ (excellent); Top Pick
New York magazine: ★★★ (generally excellent); Critics' Pick
Zagat: 28 food rating (extraordinary to perfection)
The Village Voice: Critics' Pick

Sushi Zen

108 W 44th St (bet 6th Ave and Broadway)
New York, NY 10036
(212) 302-0707

Neighborhood Map: **Midtown West/Theater District**
Category: **Japanese/Sushi**
Price Range: **$$$**
www.sushizen-ny.com

This restaurant's primo spot is the 10-seat sushi counter (with no case) that allows a limited number of diners to observe chefs at work on some of the most sublime sushi and sashimi in the city. Full bar. Serving lunch Mon–Fri, dinner Mon–Sat. Closed Sun.

The New York Times: Top Pick
Zagat: 25 food rating (very good to excellent)

NEW YORK CITY **★TOP100** Tabla/Bread Bar at Tabla

★ **BEST INDIAN IN GRAMERCY/MADISON PARK**
11 Madison Ave (near 25th St)
New York, NY 10010
(212) 889-0667

Neighborhood Map: **Gramercy/Madison Park**
Categories: **Contemporary, Indian**

Price Range: **$$$$/$$$**
www.tablany.com

Another wildly successful entry in Danny Meyer's Union Square Hospitality Group, Tabla ambitiously fuses contemporary American cuisine with heavy Indian seasoning and style. A Gramercy favorite since 1999, Tabla offers multiple distinct dining experiences, with a luxurious upstairs dining room, a popular outdoor patio, the more casual Bread Bar downstairs, and now even a street food cart that prepares Indian-inspired quick bites. Executive chef and James Beard award nominee Floyd Cardoz, a Bombay native, uses the spices of his homeland to accent fine-dining favorites. His seasonal, three-course, prix fixe menu will light up your palate with offerings such as rice-flaked halibut with a lime and watermelon curry, or the *rawa*-crusted soft shell crabs with mushrooms, fingerling potatoes and coconut *korma*. Downstairs at the Bread Bar, the tandoor oven churns out delicate breads (rosemary naan, cheese *kulcha*, smoked bacon naan) to be paired with a wide variety of chutneys and dishes such as the chicken tikka or tandoori flank steak. Vegetarian options are in abundance as well. Wash it all down with a Maharaja Pilsner or a kumquat mojito from the full bar. Reservations suggested. Main dining room serving lunch Mon–Fri, dinner nightly. Bread Bar serving lunch Mon–Sat, dinner nightly.

199

The New York Times: ★★★ (excellent); Top Pick
New York magazine: ★★★ (generally excellent); Critics' Pick
Zagat: 25 food rating (very good to excellent)
Time Out New York: Critics' Pick

Taco Taco
1726 2nd Ave (bet 89th and 90th Sts)
New York, NY 10128
(212) 289-8226

Neighborhood Map: **Upper East Side**
Categories: **Burritos, Mexican**
Price Range: **$$**

Strong margaritas, guacamole prepared tableside, Oaxacan specialties and, of course, tacos — chorizo, carnitas and even vegetarian (spinach, mushrooms and cabbage) — render this friendly, vibrant restaurant on the Upper East Side an oft-packed neighborhood favorite. Full bar. Serving lunch and dinner daily, late night Fri–Sat.

New York magazine: Critics' Pick

Tamarind

41-43 E 22nd St (bet Broadway and Park Ave S)
New York, NY 10010
(212) 674-7400

Neighborhood Map: **Gramercy/Madison Park**
Category: **Indian**
Price Range: **$$$**
www.tamarinde22.com

This sleek Indian restaurant offers a prix fixe lunch menu and special dinners of the vegetarian, mixed grill or seafood variety. Reservations required. Full bar. Serving lunch and dinner daily, late-night Fri–Sat.

The New York Times: ★★ (very good)
New York magazine: Critics' Pick
Zagat: 25 food rating (very good to excellent)
Time Out New York: Critics' Pick

200

Tanoreen

★ **BEST MIDDLE EASTERN IN BROOKLYN**
7704 3rd Ave (near 77th St)
Brooklyn, NY 11209
(718) 748-5600

Neighborhood Map: **Brooklyn (Bay Ridge)**
Categories: **Brunch, Middle Eastern**
Price Range: **$$**
www.tanoreen.com

Bay Ridge is widely considered to be a hub for some of the best Middle Eastern food in New York. Tanoreen has a lot to do with this. No alcohol available. BYOB. Serving lunch and dinner Tue–Sun. Sat–Sun brunch starting 10:30 am. Closed Mon.

The New York Times: Top Pick
New York magazine: Critics' Pick

Zagat: 26 food rating (extraordinary to perfection)
The Village Voice: Critics' Pick

Tartine

★ BEST CAFÉ IN THE WEST VILLAGE/MEATPACKING DISTRICT

253 W 11th St (near W 4th St)
New York, NY 10014
(212) 229-2611

Neighborhood Map: **West Village/Meatpacking District**
Categories: **Breakfast, Brunch, Café, French**
Price Range: **$$**

This BYOB café is so popular, you will most certainly have to wait in line to sample the delectable French fare. West Villagers love it for its charm as well as its prices. No alcohol available. BYOB. Cash only. Serving breakfast Mon–Fri, lunch and dinner nightly. Sat–Sun brunch 10:30 am–4 pm.

New York magazine: Critics' Pick
Zagat: 22 food rating (very good to excellent)
Time Out New York: Critics' Pick
The Village Voice: Critics' Pick

Tavern on Jane

31 8th Ave (near Jane St)
New York, NY 10014
(212) 675-2526

Neighborhood Map: **West Village/Meatpacking District**
Categories: **American Traditional, Brunch**
Price Range: **$$**
www.tavernonjane.com

A West Village standby for solid American Traditional favorites. Grab a beer and a burger or a glass of wine and some pasta and ease into the low-lit, laid-back mood of the place. Full bar. Serving lunch, dinner and late-night daily. Sat–Sun brunch.

Telepan

72 W 69th St (near Columbus Ave)

New York, NY 10023
(212) 580-4300

Neighborhood Map: **Upper West Side**
Categories: **Brunch, Contemporary**
Price Range: **$$$**
www.telepan-ny.com

A unique dining experience blending European flavors with
local, from-the-farm ingredients. Enjoy a meal here before
or after a show at nearby Lincoln Center. Reservations
suggested. Full bar. Serving lunch Wed–Fri, dinner nightly.
Sat–Sun brunch 11 am–2:30 pm.

The New York Times: ★★ (very good); Top Pick
New York magazine: ★★ (very good); Critics' Pick
Zagat: 25 food rating (very good to excellent)
Time Out New York: Critics' Pick
The Village Voice: Critics' Pick

Teodora

141 E 57th St (bet Lexington and 3rd Aves)
New York, NY 10022
(212) 826-7101

Neighborhood Map: **Midtown East/Murray Hill**
Category: **Italian**
Price Range: **$$$**

With specialties that hail from Italy's Emilia-Romagna region,
this casual Italian outpost features decorative touches of
homespun charm and hearty but nuanced dishes ranging from
cured meats to all manner of pastas. Reservations suggested.
Full bar. Serving lunch and dinner daily.

The New York Times: ★ (good); Top Pick
New York magazine: ★★ (very good); Critics' Pick
Zagat: 20 food rating (very good to excellent)

Tía Pol

★ **BEST SMALL PLATES IN CHELSEA**
205 10th Ave (bet 22nd and 23rd Sts)
New York, NY 10011
(212) 675-8805

Neighborhood Map: **Chelsea**
Categories: **Brunch, Small Plates, Spanish, Wine Bar**
Price Range: **$$**
www.tiapol.com

This narrow Chelsea wine bar with a small dining room in the back serves some of the best Spanish small plates in town to an affluent crowd. Try the *pescado en adobo* (crispy marinated fish). And a glass of sangria couldn't hurt. Beer, wine and sangria available. Serving lunch Tue–Fri, dinner nightly. Sat–Sun brunch 11 am–3 pm.

The New York Times: Top Pick
New York magazine: ★ (good); Critics' Pick
Zagat: 24 food rating (very good to excellent)
Time Out New York: Critics' Pick

Tides Seafood

★ **BEST SEAFOOD ON THE LOWER EAST SIDE**
102 Norfolk St (near Delancey St)
New York, NY 10002
(212) 254-8855

Neighborhood Map: **Lower East Side**
Category: **Seafood**
Price Range: **$$**
www.tidesseafood.com/1.html

Known for its lobster rolls, Tides is a refreshing touch of the sea — the ceiling is made of bamboo sticks in rolling wave formation — in Lower Manhattan. Reservations suggested. Beer and wine available. Serving dinner Tue–Sun. Closed Mon.

Zagat: 24 food rating (very good to excellent)

Tocqueville

★ **BEST FRENCH IN UNION SQUARE/FLATIRON**
1 E 15th St (near 5th Ave)
New York, NY 10003
(212) 647-1515

Neighborhood Map: **Union Square/Flatiron**
Categories: **Contemporary, French**
Price Range: **$$$**

www.tocquevillerestaurant.com

Sophisticated French-American cuisine, creative cocktails (passion fruit sake *caipirinha*, mint juniper) and a luxe, white-tablecloth dining space. Reservations suggested. Full bar. Serving lunch and dinner Mon–Sat. Closed Sun.

The New York Times: ★★ (very good)
New York magazine: Critics' Pick
Zagat: 25 food rating (very good to excellent)

Tom's Restaurant

★ **BEST DINER IN BROOKLYN**
782 Washington Ave (near Sterling Pl)
Brooklyn, NY 11238
(718) 636-9738

Neighborhood Map: **Brooklyn (Prospect Heights)**
Categories: **Breakfast, Burgers, Diner**
Price Range: **$**

If you're looking for a real New York diner, Tom's is your spot. Opened in 1936, this Prospect Heights institution is legendary for its friendly service, pancakes, omelets and soda fountain specialties. No alcohol available. Cash only. Serving breakfast and lunch Mon–Sat. Closed Sun.

The New York Times: Top Pick
Zagat: 20 food rating (very good to excellent)

NEW YORK CITY
★TOP100 Town
15 W 56th St (near 5th Ave, Chambers Hotel)
New York, NY 10019
(212) 582-4445

Neighborhood Map: **Midtown West/Theater District**
Categories: **Breakfast, Brunch, Contemporary, Hotel Restaurant**
Price Range: **$$$**
www.townrestaurant.com

Trendy restaurants in four-star hotels can have a short shelf life, but Town has proven to have sticking power since opening in 2001, thanks in large part to a hefty dose of class and innovative yet classic fine-dining cuisine. This gorgeous, three-tiered space, designed by the Rockwell Group, features plush, upholstered walls and 24-foot ceilings. Expense accounters, tastemakers and beautiful people of all types can be found in the dining room, the balcony or the upstairs bar, where mixologist extraordinaire Albert Trummer concocts creative champagne drinks, raspberry martinis and Singapore slings. Chef Geoffrey Zakarian's menu, which changes monthly, is similarly ambitious, but not overly so, with escargot risotto, foie gras terrine or roasted black cod. Chocolate and vanilla beignets or the chocolate soufflé for two prove difficult to resist. Full bar. Serving breakfast, lunch and dinner daily. Sun brunch 11 am–2:30 pm.

The New York Times: ★★★ (excellent); Top Pick
New York magazine: ★★★ (generally excellent); Critics' Pick
Zagat: 24 food rating (very good to excellent)
Time Out New York: Critics' Pick

NEW YORK CITY
★TOP100 **Turkish Kitchen**

★ **BEST TURKISH IN NYC**

205

386 3rd Ave (bet 27th and 28th Sts)
New York, NY 10016
(212) 679-6633

Neighborhood Map: **Gramercy/Madison Park**
Categories: **Brunch, Small Plates, Turkish**
Price Range: **$$**
www.turkishkitchen.com

This place looks more like one of those trendy, newfangled sushi bars — shiny surfaces, bright colors, sleek lines — than a restaurant offering traditional Turkish fare, but one look at the clientele, heavily Turkish and Greek, confirms its bona fides. And if that weren't reason enough to visit, there are, of course, the exceptional food and attentive service. Those keen on small plates will enjoy the extensive menu of hot and cold *mezes*. The cold list includes several variations of eggplant and house-made yogurt with cucumber. And the hot appetizers include pan-fried calf's liver served with onion and parsley mix and poached beef dumplings with garlic yogurt sauce (both favorites of *New York Times* food critic Frank Bruni). Grilled chicken, baked lamb shank and whole grilled sea bass populate the entrée list. Desserts include the typically mouth-watering, honey-drenched,

pistachio-crusted pastries for which the Turks are known.
Reservations suggested. Full bar. Serving lunch Mon–Fri, dinner
nightly. Sun brunch 11 am–3 pm.

The New York Times: Top Pick
Zagat: 22 food rating (very good to excellent)
Time Out New York: Critics' Pick

---

24 Prince

★ BEST AMERICAN TRADITIONAL IN LITTLE ITALY/NOLITA

24 Prince St (bet Mott and Elizabeth Sts)
New York, NY 10012
(212) 226-8624

Neighborhood Map: **Little Italy/NoLita**
Categories: **American Traditional, Brunch**
Price Range: **$$**
www.24prince.com

Traditional American food gets dressed up in this fashionable
and chic setting. Full bar. Serving lunch Tue–Fri, dinner
nightly, late-night Fri–Sat. Sat–Sun brunch noon–3:30 pm.

The New York Times: Top Pick

★TOP100 Union Square Cafe

★ BEST CONTEMPORARY IN NYC

21 E 16th St (near Union Square W)
New York, NY 10003
(212) 243-4020

Neighborhood Map: **Union Square/Flatiron**
Category: **Contemporary**
Price Range: **$$$**
www.unionsquarecafe.com

Rome wasn't built in a day, nor was the far reach of Danny
Meyer's restaurant group. It all started with Union Square
Cafe, which opened in 1985 and has remained among the
city's most popular and beloved restaurants year after year.
This James Beard award-winning restaurant (in multiple
categories over the years) was also a torchbearer for the
locally grown, seasonally sustainable movement: The Union

206

Square Greenmarket supplies the kitchen. Whether you're a 20-year devotee of the lobster shepherd's pie (one of the daily specials) or just grabbing a burger at the bar — a good spot to snag if you don't have a reservation — USC pleases all palates with warm service, its casually elegant dining room and "American cuisine with an Italian soul." Consistency is king, as chef/partner Michael Romano has been with the restaurant since 1988. The signature tuna steak with wasabi-mashed potatoes remains on the menu in addition to a selection of pastas and entrées such as lamb chops and crispy duck confit. Reservations suggested. Full bar with award-winning wine list. Serving lunch and dinner daily.

The New York Times: ★★★ (excellent); Top Pick
New York magazine: ★★★ (generally excellent); Critics' Pick
Zagat: 27 food rating (extraordinary to perfection)

NEW YORK CITY
★TOP100 **Veritas**

43 E 20th St (bet Broadway and Park Ave S)
New York, NY 10003
(212) 353-3700

Neighborhood Map: **Union Square/Flatiron**
Category: **Contemporary**
Price Range: **$$$$$**
www.veritas-nyc.com

At this Mobil-Three-Star-rated restaurant in Flatiron, the exceptional menu of both contemporary American and French-leaning entrées is the background music to the sound of happy oenophiles clinking glasses and toasting a cellar stocked with 192,000 bottles of more than 3,000 wines. But Veritas, which opened in 1998 and draws from the private cellars of restaurant owner Park B. Smith, is not merely a haven for smug wine sophisticates. Renowned wine director Timothy Kopec and his team of sommeliers happily field questions and offer suggestions, making the experience here approachable and enjoyable even for those who think Châteauneuf-du-Pape is just a castle ruin in France. French-trained chef Grégory Pugin offers three-course and six-course tasting menus and manages to wow diners who may have come solely for the wine with such artfully prepared fare as Dover sole Provençal, venison and lobster *nage*. Though we don't know why you'd want to, you can forgo the extensive Bordeaux collection and get a gin and tonic here, too (i.e., full bar.) Reservations suggested. Serving light fare 3 pm–5:30 pm Mon–Fri, dinner nightly.

Michelin Guide: ★ (a very good restaurant in its category)
The New York Times: ★★★ (excellent)
New York magazine: ★★★ (generally excellent); Critics' Pick
Zagat: 26 food rating (extraordinary to perfection)
Time Out New York: Critics' Pick

Veselka
144 2nd Ave (near 9th St)
New York, NY 10003
(212) 228-9682

Neighborhood Map: **East Village/NoHo**
Categories: **Breakfast, Brunch, Ukrainian**
Price Range: **$$**
www.veselka.com

For over 50 years, Veselka has provided a taste of the Ukraine to East Village late-night noshers. Borscht (hot or cold), blintzes, grilled kielbasa and breakfast sandwiches are available 24 hours. Beer and wine available. Open 24 hours.

Zagat: 18 (good to very good)

Wall Street Burger Shoppe
30 Water St (bet Broad St and Coenties Slip)
New York, NY 10004
(212) 425-1000

Neighborhood Map: **Financial District**
Category: **Burgers**
Price Range: **$$**
www.burgershoppenyc.com

The casual fare here includes great burgers, bar snacks and salads, plus local brews on tap upstairs. Beer and wine available. Serving lunch, dinner and late-night Mon–Sat. Closed Sun.

NEW YORK CITY
★TOP100 wd-50

★ BEST CONTEMPORARY ON THE LOWER EAST SIDE
50 Clinton St (bet Stanton and Rivington Sts)

New York, NY 10002
(212) 477-2900

Neighborhood Map: **Lower East Side**
Category: **Contemporary**
Price Range: **$$$**
www.wd-50.com

Like some deranged experiment — that's gone horribly right
— from a mad scientist's culinary laboratory, wd-50 rewards
adventurous diners with food that's beyond complex, but fun
at heart. This Lower East Side dining room is simple, warm
and comfortable, with a fireplace and cozy booths, perhaps
to contrast a cuisine that's full of surprises. The man behind
the molecular madness, Wylie Dufresne, a James Beard
Foundation Best Chef: New York nominee, trained under
the venerable Jean-Georges Vongerichten before opening
this 70-seat restaurant bearing his initials in 2003. You'll find
everything from smoked eel with guava and puffed yuzu to
Wagyu flat iron steak with coffee gnocchi. The tasting menu
(with optional wine pairings) is full of aesthetically amusing
edibles such as beef tongue, yellowtail tartare, the chef's
space-age take on eggs Benedict and toasted coconut cake
to finish. Reservations suggested. Full bar. Serving lunch
Wed–Fri, dinner nightly.

Michelin Guide: ★ (a very good restaurant in its category)
The New York Times: ★★★ (excellent); Top Pick
New York magazine: ★★★★ (exceptional; consistently
  elite); Critics' Pick
Zagat: 23 food rating (very good to excellent)
Time Out New York: Critics' Pick

Westville/Westville East

**★ BEST AMERICAN TRADITIONAL IN THE EAST
  VILLAGE/NOHO**
Neighborhood Map: **East Village/NoHo**
173 Ave A (near 11th St)
New York, NY 10009
(212) 677-2933

**★ BEST AMERICAN TRADITIONAL IN THE WEST
  VILLAGE/MEATPACKING DISTRICT**
Neighborhood Map: **West Village/Meatpacking District**
210 W 10th St (bet Bleecker and W 4th Sts)

New York, NY 10014
(212) 741-7971

Categories: **American Traditional, Bakery, Brunch**
Price Range: **$$**
www.westvillenyc.com/about.aspx

Westville's tiny dining room (the East Village location is bigger)
with an open storefront and chalkboard menus specializes
in clever renditions of home-cooked classics and plenty of
vegetables. Niman Ranch beef hot dogs, a burger on a thick
Portuguese muffin, or mac and cheese all go superbly with a
glass of mint lemonade. Beer and wine available. Serving lunch
and dinner daily. Sat–Sun brunch.

New York magazine: Critics' Pick
Zagat: 22 food rating (very good to excellent)

WonJo

23 W 32nd St (near 5th Ave)
New York, NY 10001
(212) 695-5815

Neighborhood Map: **Garment District**
Categories: **Dumplings, Japanese/Sushi, Korean**
Price Range: **$$**
www.wonjo32.com

Open 24 hours a day, Koreatown's WonJo, a local favorite,
specializes in Korean barbecue as well as other traditional
Korean dishes. Don't miss the dumplings. Full bar. Open
24 hours.

Zagat: 20 food rating (very good to excellent)

NEW YORK CITY
★TOP100 Woo Lae Oak

★ BEST KOREAN IN NYC
148 Mercer St (bet Houston and Prince Sts)
New York, NY 10012
(212) 925-8200

Neighborhood Map: **SoHo**
Category: **Korean**

Price Range: **$$$**
www.woolaeoaksoho.com

Why leave grilling to the professionals when you can let the professionals leave it to you? At trendy Woo Lae Oak, a West Coast transplant in SoHo (formerly in Midtown), each table comes equipped with a gas grill in the middle for an entertaining, interactive dining experience. Just don't get carried away with the *soju* (Korea's answer to sake) if you don't want to singe your silk shirt or dangling wrist accessories. You can barbecue anything from tiger prawns, sliced rib eye and spicy pork tenderloin to swordfish filet and ostrich. Leave the heavy lifting to the kitchen, though, which prepares a number of contemporary Korean dishes. Starters include ahi tartare and flash-fried calamari, while entrées range from classics such as *bi bim bop* to the *kal bi jim*, beef short rib simmered in sake, ginger and soy glaze. Full bar. Serving lunch and dinner daily.

The New York Times: ★★ (very good)
Zagat: 22 food rating (very good to excellent)

Yakitori Totto

251 W 55th St, 2nd Fl (bet Broadway and 8th Ave)
New York, NY 10019
(212) 245-4555

Neighborhood Map: **Midtown West/Theater District**
Category: **Japanese/Sushi**
Price Range: **$**
www.torysnyc.com/totto.htm

Chicken on a skewer (yakitori) is the specialty here, though many different kinds of meat and other traditional Japanese dishes are served. Be prepared to wait, as locals truly line up to get in. Reservations suggested. Beer, wine and sake available. Serving dinner nightly, late-night Mon–Sat.

The New York Times: Top Pick
Zagat: 26 food rating (extraordinary to perfection)

Zabar's Cafe

★ **BEST GOURMET TAKEOUT ON THE UPPER WEST SIDE**
2245 Broadway (near 80th St)

New York, NY 10024
(212) 787-2000

Neighborhood Map: **Upper West Side**
Categories: **Bagels, Bakery, Breakfast, Deli, Gourmet
    Takeout**
Price Range: **$**
www.zabars.com

This famous, quintessentially New York gourmet grocery
supplies the Upper West Side with meats, cheeses, smoked
fish and other essentials. The adjoining café doles out
countless bagels and lox (as well as other breakfast specials,
sandwiches and grilled panini) to the crowds. No alcohol
available. Serving breakfast, lunch and early dinner daily.

Zagat: 19 food rating (good to very good)

Zaitzeff
Neighborhood Map: **East Village/NoHo**
18 Ave B (bet 2nd and 3rd Sts)
New York, NY 10009
(212) 477-7137

★ **BEST BURGERS IN THE FINANCIAL DISTRICT**
Neighborhood Map: **Financial District**
72 Nassau St (near John St)
New York, NY 10038
(212) 571-7272

Categories: **Breakfast, Burgers**
Price Range: **$$**
www.zaitzeffnyc.com

American-style Kobe beef burgers and a full bar (at the Avenue
B location). Need we say more? Beer and wine available at
Financial District location. Serving breakfast, lunch and dinner
daily. Closes earlier Sat–Sun.

New York magazine: Critics' Pick

Zoma
★ **BEST AFRICAN IN HARLEM**
2084 Frederick Douglass Blvd (near 113th St)

New York, NY 10026
(212) 662-0620

Neighborhood Map: **Harlem**
Category: **African**
Price Range: **$$**
www.zomanyc.com

Break out the *injera* and soak up some spice at Zoma in Harlem, where you'll find some of the finest Ethiopian cuisine in the city. Reservations suggested. Full bar. Cash only. Serving lunch Fri–Sun, dinner nightly.

Zagat: 23 food rating (very good to excellent)
Time Out New York: Critics' Pick

213

NEIGHBORHOOD MAPS

215

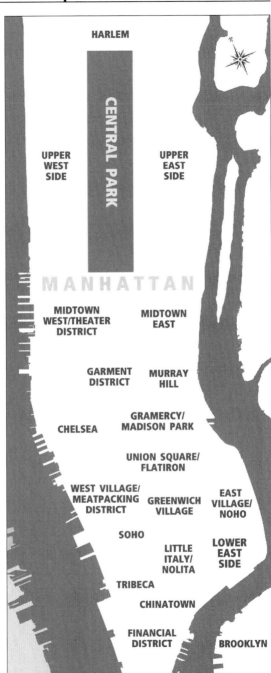

A GUIDE TO THE BEST RESTAURANTS

CHELSEA

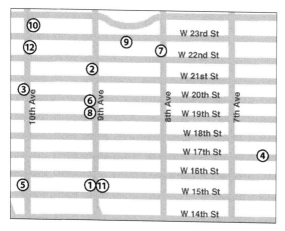

1. **AMY'S BREAD**
2. **BILLY'S BAKERY**
3. **COOKSHOP**
4. **DA UMBERTO**
5. **DEL POSTO**
6. **LA BERGAMOTE**
7. **MURRAY'S BAGELS**
8. **OMAI**
9. **PATSY'S PIZZERIA**
10. **THE RED CAT**
11. **SARABETH'S**
12. **TÍA POL**

CHINATOWN

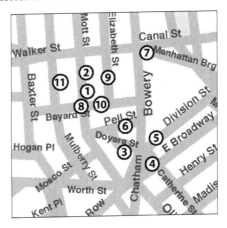

1. **AMAZING 66**
2. **BIG WONG**
3. **DOYERS VIETNAMESE**
4. **FOOD SING 88 CORP.**
5. **FULEEN SEAFOOD**
6. **JOE'S SHANGHAI**
7. **JUMBO HOT DOGS**
8. **NEW BO KY**
9. **ORIENTAL GARDEN**
10. **THE ORIGINAL CHINATOWN ICE CREAM FACTORY**
11. **PHO VIET HUONG**

EAST VILLAGE/NOHO

NEIGHBORHOOD MAPS

219

1. **ANGELICA KITCHEN**
2. **ANGON ON THE SIXTH**
3. **B & H DAIRY RESTAURANT**
4. **BACK FORTY**
5. **CAFE MOGADOR**
6. **CARACAS AREPA BAR**
7. **DEGUSTATION WINE & TASTING BAR**
8. **DESSERT TRUCK (NIGHTTIME LOCATION)**
9. **DUMPLING MAN**
10. **HEARTH**
11. **HOLY BASIL**
12. **HUMMUS PLACE**
13. **MAMOUN'S**
14. **MOMOFUKU NOODLE BAR**
15. **MOMOFUKU SSÄM BAR**
16. **MOUSTACHE**
17. **PRUNE**
18. **PYLOS**
19. **VESELKA**
20. **WESTVILLE EAST**
21. **ZAITZEFF**

FINANCIAL DISTRICT

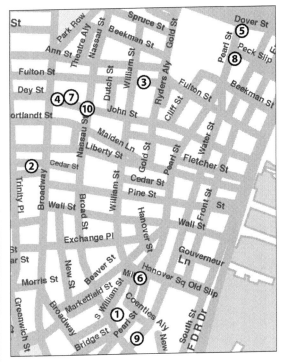

1. **ADRIENNE'S PIZZABAR**
2. **ALAN'S FALAFEL (FOOD CART)**
3. **BENNIE'S THAI CAFE**
4. **BREAD & OLIVE**
5. **BRIDGE CAFE**
6. **HARRY'S CAFE AND STEAK**
7. **LES HALLES**
8. **MARKJOSEPH STEAKHOUSE**
9. **WALL STREET BURGER SHOPPE**
10. **ZAITZEFF**

GARMENT DISTRICT

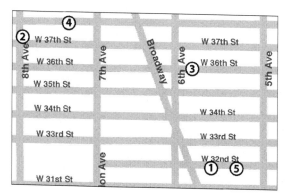

1. **GAHM MI OAK**
2. **GRAY'S PAPAYA**
3. **KEENS STEAKHOUSE**
4. **LAZZARA'S PIZZA CAFE**
5. **WONJO**

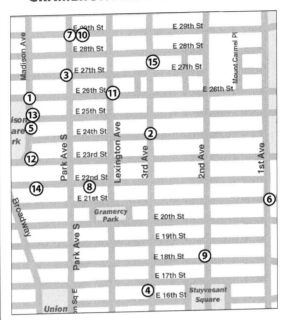

WHERE THE LOCALS EAT™

GRAMERCY/MADISON PARK

222

1. **A VOCE**
2. **BAR MILANO**
3. **BLUE SMOKE**
4. **CHINO'S**
5. **ELEVEN MADISON PARK**
6. **ESS-A-BAGEL**
7. **LES HALLES**
8. **NOVITÁ**
9. **POSTO**
10. **RESTO**
11. **SARAVANAAS**
12. **SHAKE SHACK**
13. **TABLA/BREAD BAR AT TABLA**
14. **TAMARIND**
15. **TURKISH KITCHEN**

GREENWICH VILLAGE

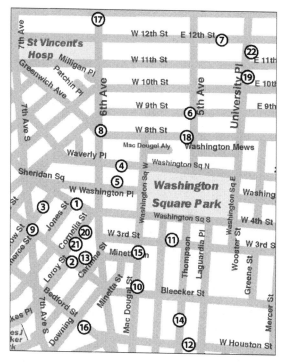

1. **AKI**
2. **AMY'S BREAD**
3. **ANNISA**
4. **BABBO**
5. **BLUE HILL**
6. **CRU**
7. **GOTHAM BAR AND GRILL**
8. **GRAY'S PAPAYA**
9. **HUMMUS PLACE**
10. **HUMMUS PLACE**
11. **IL MULINO**
12. **JANE**
13. **JOE'S PIZZA**
14. **LUPA**
15. **MAMOUN'S**
16. **MAS**

17. **MURRAY'S BAGELS**
18. **OTTO**
19. **PATSY'S PIZZERIA**
20. **PEARL OYSTER BAR**
21. **PO**
22. **SAIGON GRILL**

223

HARLEM

WEST MAP

go to
151st St

1. **A TASTE OF SEAFOOD**

2. **AFRICA KINE**

3. **AMY RUTH'S**

4. **CHARLES' SOUTHERN-STYLE KITCHEN**

5. **DINOSAUR BAR-B-QUE**

6. **LA FONDA BORICUA**

7. **PATSY'S PIZZERIA (ORIGINAL)**

8. **SETTEPANI BAKERY**

9. **STRICTLY ROOTS**

10. **ZOMA**

EAST MAP

HARLEM

W 131st St
W 130th St
W 129th St
W 128th St
W 127th St
126th St
124th St
123rd St
122nd St
121st St
120th St
119th St
118th St
117th St

E 131st
E 130th
E 129th St
E 128th St
E 127th St

Dr Martin L King Jr Blvd

E 13ist

FDR Dr
FDR Dr S
369th Harlem

E 129th St
E 128th St
E 127th St
E 126th St
E 125th St
E 124th St
E 123rd St
E 122nd St
E 121st St
E 120th St
E 119th St
E 118th St
E 117th St

E 124th

Marcus Garvey Memorial Park

Mt Morris Park W

Malcolm Blvd

W 116th St
Luis Munoz Marin Blvd
E 115th St

E 116th St

Lenox Ave

5th Ave

Tony Mendez Pl

W 111th St
E 111th St
Central Park N
Tito Puente Way

E 113th St
E 112th St

E 111th St

Central Park

Harlem Mere

Park Dr

Madison Ave

Park Ave

E 108th St
E 107th St
E 106th St

E 110th St
E 109th St
E 108th St

225

LITTLE ITALY/NOLITA

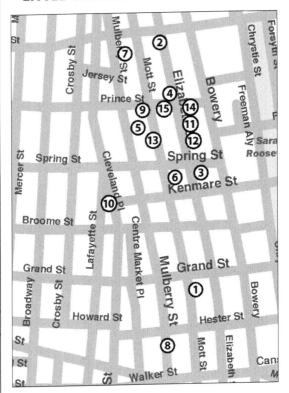

1. BÁNH MÌ SAIGON BAKERY
2. CAFE COLONIAL
3. CAFE EL PORTAL
4. CAFÉ HABANA
5. EIGHT MILE CREEK
6. EPISTROPHY
7. GHENET
8. IL CORTILE
9. THE KITCHEN CLUB
10. LA ESQUINA
11. LOVELY DAY
12. PEASANT
13. PINCHE TAQUERIA
14. PUBLIC
15. 24 PRINCE

A GUIDE TO THE BEST RESTAURANTS

LOWER EAST SIDE

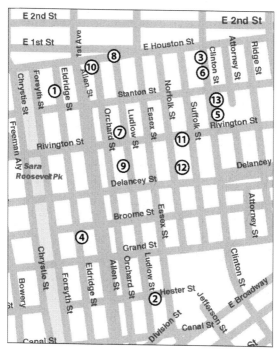

1. ÁPIZZ
2. BROWN CAFÉ
3. CLINTON ST. BAKING COMPANY & RESTAURANT
4. DUMPLING HOUSE
5. FALAI
6. FRANKIES 17 SPUNTINO
7. 'INOTECA
8. KATZ'S DELICATESSEN
9. KUMA INN
10. RUSS & DAUGHTERS
11. SCHILLER'S LIQUOR BAR
12. TIDES SEAFOOD
13. WD-50

MIDTOWN EAST/MURRAY HILL

NEW YORK, NEW YORK

1. ALTO
2. AMMA
3. AQUAVIT
4. ARTISANAL
5. AVRA
6. BLT STEAK
7. CARL'S STEAKS
8. DAWAT
9. DESSERT TRUCK (DAYTIME LOCATION)
10. ESS-A-BAGEL
11. FELIDIA
12. THE FOUR SEASONS
13. HATSUHANA
14. HATSUHANA
15. L'ATELIER DE JOËL ROBUCHON
16. LA GIOCONDA
17. LA GRENOUILLE
18. MURRAY HILL DINER
19. OCEANA
20. PAMPANO
21. PATSY'S PIZZERIA
22. ROSA MEXICANO
23. SAKAGURA
24. SARGE'S DELI
25. 2ND AVE DELI
26. SHUN LEE PALACE
27. SMITH & WOLLENSKY
28. SPARKS STEAK HOUSE
29. SUSHI YASUDA
30. TEODORA

229

MIDTOWN WEST/THEATER DISTRICT

1. AMY'S BREAD
2. AZURI CAFE
3. BECCO
4. BLUE RIBBON SUSHI BAR & GRILL
5. BREAD & OLIVE
6. BURGER JOINT AT LE PARKER MERIDIEN
7. DB BISTRO MODERNE
8. EATERY
9. ESCA
10. ESTIATORIO MILOS
11. INSIEME
12. ISLAND BURGERS & SHAKES
13. JOE'S SHANGHAI
14. LA BERGAMOTE
15. LANDMARC
16. LAZZARA'S PIZZA CAFE
17. LAZZARA'S PIZZA CAFE

18. LE BERNARDIN
19. MASA
20. THE MODERN
21. MOLYVOS
22. NORMA'S
23. PER SE
24. PIANO DUE
25. RICE 'N' BEANS
26. SARABETH'S
27. SUGIYAMA
28. SUSHI OF GARI
29. SUSHI ZEN
30. TOWN
31. YAKITORI TOTTO

A GUIDE TO THE BEST RESTAURANTS

SOHO

1. **ALIDORO**
2. **AQUAGRILL**
3. **BALTHAZAR**
4. **BLUE RIBBON BRASSERIE**
5. **BLUE RIBBON SUSHI**
6. **FIAMMA**
7. **KITTICHAI**
8. **L'ECOLE**
9. **LUCKY STRIKE**
10. **LURE FISHBAR**
11. **MOONCAKE FOODS**
12. **OMEN**
13. **RAOUL'S**
14. **SAVOY**
15. **SNACK**
16. **WOO LAE OAK**

TRIBECA

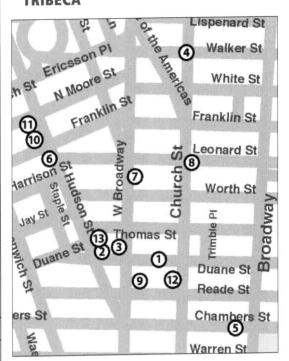

1. BLAUE GANS
2. BOULEY
3. BOULEY UPSTAIRS
4. BREAD TRIBECA
5. CARL'S STEAKS
6. CHANTERELLE
7. LANDMARC
8. MATSUGEN
9. NAM
10. NOBU
11. NOBU NEXT DOOR
12. PAKISTAN TEA HOUSE
13. SCALINI FEDELI

UNION SQUARE/FLATIRON

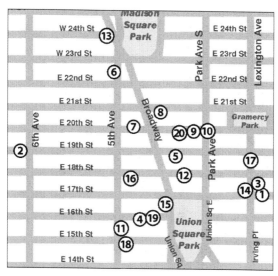

1. **BAR JAMÓN**
2. **BOQUERIA**
3. **CASA MONO**
4. **CHAT 'N CHEW**
5. **CRAFT**
6. **EISENBERG'S SANDWICH SHOP**
7. **FLEUR DE SEL**
8. **GIORGIO'S OF GRAMERCY**
9. **GRAMERCY TAVERN**
10. **L'EXPRESS**
11. **MESA GRILL**
12. **OLD TOWN BAR & RESTAURANT**
13. **OTTIMO**
14. **PURE FOOD AND WINE**
15. **REPUBLIC**
16. **ROSA MEXICANO**
17. **71 IRVING PLACE COFFEE & TEA BAR**
18. **TOCQUEVILLE**
19. **UNION SQUARE CAFE**
20. **VERITAS**

UPPER EAST SIDE

A GUIDE TO THE BEST RESTAURANTS

NEW YORK, NEW YORK

1. ATLANTIC GRILL
2. AUREOLE
3. BEYOGLU
4. CAFÉ BOULUD
5. CANDLE CAFE
6. CANDLE 79
7. DANIEL
8. DAVIDBURKE & DONATELLA
9. DONGURI
10. EJ'S LUNCHEONETTE
11. ERMINIA
12. ETATS-UNIS
13. ITHAKA
14. JOJO
15. LAND NORTHEAST THAI
16. PAOLA'S
17. PATSY'S PIZZERIA
18. PATSY'S PIZZERIA
19. PAYARD PATISSERIE & BISTRO
20. SABLE'S
21. SARABETH'S
22. SARABETH'S
23. SETTE MEZZO
24. SUSHI OF GARI
25. TACO TACO

UPPER WEST SIDE

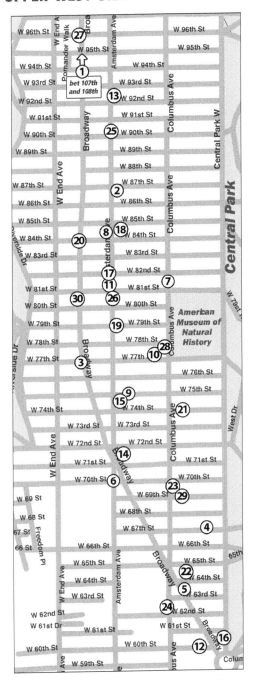

W 96th St · W End A · Broa · Amsterdam Ave · W 96th St
(27) · W 95th St · W 95th St
W 94th St · (1) · W 94th St · Columbus Ave · Central Park W
W 93rd St · bet 107th and 108th · W 93rd St
W 92nd St · (13) W 92nd St
W 91st St · W 91st St
W 90th St · (25) W 90th St
W 89th St · W 89th St
W End Ave · W 88th St
W 87th St · (2) W 87th St
W 86th St · W 86th St · Columbus Ave
W 85th St · W 85th St
W 84th St · (8)(18) W 84th St · Central Park
(20) · W 83rd St
W 83rd St · Amsterdam Ave
W 82nd St
(17) · W 82nd St
W 81st St · (11) · W 81st St · (7)
(30) · (26) · American
W 80th St · W 80th St · Museum of
(19) · W 79th St · Natural
W 79th St · History
W 78th St · W 78th St
Broadway · (28)
W 77th St · (3) · W 77th St · (10)
W 76th St
(9) · W 75th St
(15) · W 74th St
W 74th St · (21)
W 73rd St · Columbus Ave · West Dr
W 72nd St
W End Ave · W 72nd St
(14)
W 71st St · W 71st St
(6) · W 70th St
W 70th St · (23)
W 69 St · (29)
W 68 St · (4)
67 St · W 67th St
66 St · Freedom Pl · W 66th St
W 65th St · (22) W 65th St · 65th
W End Ave · W 64th St · (5) W 64th St
Amsterdam Ave · W 63rd St
W 62nd St · (24) W 62nd St
W 61st Dr · W 61st St · (16)
W 60th St · (12)
W 59th St · Colu

A GUIDE TO THE BEST RESTAURANTS

NEW YORK, NEW YORK

1. ABSOLUTE BAGELS
2. BARNEY GREENGRASS
3. BIG NICK'S BURGER AND PIZZA JOINT
4. CAFÉ DES ARTISTES
5. CAFE FIORELLO
6. CAFE LUXEMBOURG
7. CALLE OCHO
8. CELESTE
9. 'CESCA
10. DOVETAIL
11. EJ'S LUNCHEONETTE
12. GABRIEL'S BAR & RESTAURANT
13. GENNARO
14. GRAY'S PAPAYA
15. HUMMUS PLACE
16. JEAN GEORGES
17. LAND THAI KITCHEN
18. THE NEPTUNE ROOM
19. NICE MATIN
20. OUEST
21. PATSY'S PIZZERIA
22. PICHOLINE
23. RIGOLETTO PIZZA
24. ROSA MEXICANO
25. SAIGON GRILL
26. SARABETH'S
27. SUPER TACOS
28. SUSHI OF GARI
29. TELEPAN
30. ZABAR'S CAFE

WEST VILLAGE/MEATPACKING DISTRICT

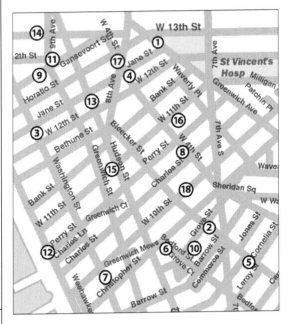

238

1. **A SALT & BATTERY**
2. **A.O.C.**
3. **BARBUTO**
4. **CORNER BISTRO**
5. **FAICCO'S**
6. **THE LITTLE OWL**
7. **MALATESTA TRATTORIA**
8. **MARY'S FISH CAMP**
9. **MERKATO 55**
10. **MOUSTACHE**
11. **PASTIS**
12. **PERRY ST**
13. **PICCOLO ANGOLO**
14. **SPICE MARKET**
15. **THE SPOTTED PIG**
16. **TARTINE**
17. **TAVERN ON JANE**
18. **WESTVILLE**

BROOKLYN MAPS KEY

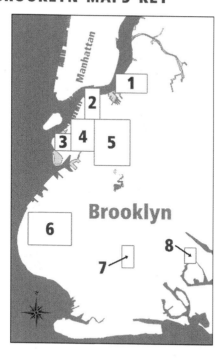

BROOKLYN MAP 1: WILLAMSBURG

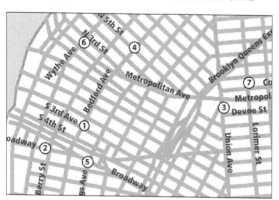

1. **BONITA**
2. **DINER**
3. **DUMONT**
4. **EGG**
5. **PETER LUGER STEAK HOUSE**
6. **RELISH**
7. **SETTEPANI BAKERY**

BROOKLYN MAP 2: DUMBO AND BROOKLYN HEIGHTS

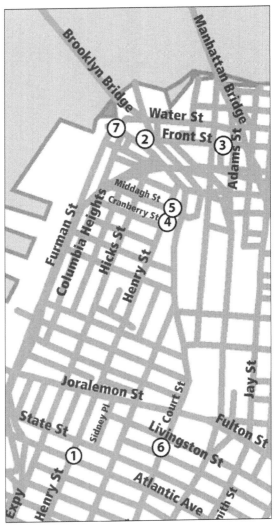

240

1. **CHIPSHOP**
2. **FIVE FRONT**
3. **HECHO EN DUMBO**
4. **HENRY'S END**
5. **NOODLE PUDDING**
6. **QUEEN RESTAURANT**
7. **THE RIVER CAFÉ**

BROOKLYN MAP 3: RED HOOK

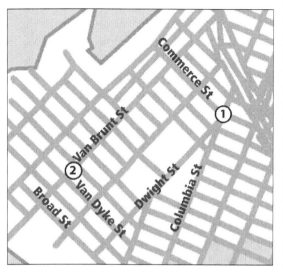

1. **DEFONTE'S**
2. **THE GOOD FORK**

BROOKLYN MAP 4: CARROLL GARDENS AND BOERUM HILL

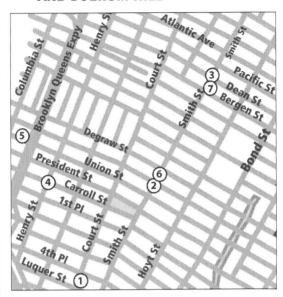

1. **FRANKIES 457 SPUNTINO**
2. **THE GROCERY**
3. **KI SUSHI**
4. **LUCALI**
5. **PETITE CREVETTE**
6. **PO**
7. **SAUL**

BROOKLYN MAP 5: PARK SLOPE, FORT GREENE, CLINTON HILL AND PROSPECT HEIGHTS

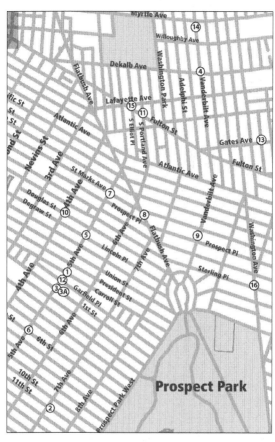

1.	**AL DI LA**	**9.**	**GARDEN CAFE**
2.	**APPLEWOOD**	**10.**	**GHENET**
3.	**BLUE RIBBON BRASSERIE**	**11.**	**HABANA OUTPOST**
3A.	**BLUE RIBBON SUSHI**	**12.**	**LA VILLA PIZZERIA**
4.	**BONITA**	**13.**	**LOCANDA VINI & OLII**
5.	**BROOKLYN FISH CAMP**	**14.**	**LUZ**
6.	**CHIPSHOP**	**15.**	**THE SMOKE JOINT**
7.	**CONVIVIUM OSTERIA**	**16.**	**TOM'S RESTAURANT**
8.	**FRANNY'S**		

BROOKLYN MAP 6: BAY RIDGE AND DYKER HEIGHTS

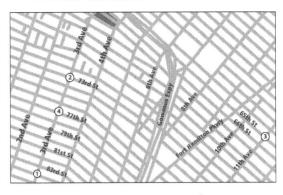

1. **AREO**
2. **CHIPSHOP**
3. **FAICCO'S**
4. **TANOREEN**

BROOKLYN MAP 7: MIDWOOD

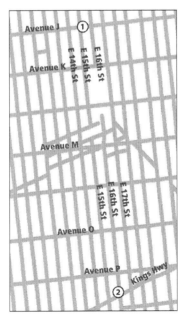

1. **DI FARA PIZZA**
2. **JOE'S PIZZA**

BROOKLYN MAP 8: MILL BASIN

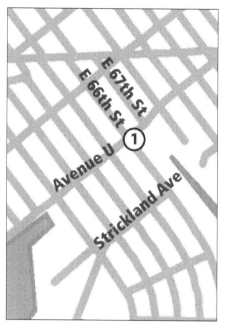

1.   LA VILLA PIZZERIA

WHERE THE LOCALS EAT™

RESTAURANT INDEX
ALPHABETICAL

A GUIDE TO THE BEST RESTAURANTS

247

RESTAURANT INDEX

248

NEW YORK, NEW YORK

About Us

At Where The Locals Eat, we get indigestion just thinking about relying on public opinion polls — they capture Olive Garden devotees and deep-fried-cheese addicts — to identify the best restaurants in a city. We love democracy as much as the next guy, but not when it comes to the serious business of determining culinary chops.

No, we prefer an authoritative approach, balancing lengthy surveys of serious diners and hopelessly hooked restaurant habitues with the opinions and extensive research of certified foodies. Ultimately, our discerning brood devises weighted, meticulously researched, ever-changing and commanding guides to the best 100 restaurants in each of the largest 50 cities in the United States, including best-of winners in any number of dining categories. We celebrate the best diners right alongside extravagant, multi-course destinations where questions are popped and anniversary memories are made, the tastiest rathskeller sausage on the same page as the organic vegetarian café.

The idea behind Where The Locals Eat is to *guide* not to *list*. We'll guide you to places that aren't just great when the owner's around or when the one talented chef is in the kitchen, and we'll guide you to reliable comfort food and ethnic finds not much known outside the neighborhood. You won't be overwhelmed by more restaurants than you can try in a lifetime, just the handful of great restaurants right near you, wherever you may be.

So get our take on your treasured trattoria or discover some out-of-the-way spots you'd never have found on your own. Simply settle in and find great restaurants.

And when you get there, tell them a local sent you.

Pat Embry
Editorial Director
Magellan Press